# ALL I NEED IS

# JESUS
### & A GOOD PAIR OF JEANS

# ALL I NEED IS

# JESUS

## & A GOOD PAIR OF JEANS

the tired supergirl's search for grace

## susanna foth aughtmon

Revell

*a division of Baker Publishing Group*
Grand Rapids, Michigan

© 2009 by Susanna Foth Aughtmon

Published by Revell
a division of Baker Publishing Group
P.O. Box 6287, Grand Rapids, MI 49516-6287
www.revellbooks.com

Printed in the United States of America

Library of Congress Cataloging-in-Publication Data
Aughtmon, Susanna Foth, 1970–
    All I need is Jesus and a good pair of jeans : the tired supergirl's search for
    grace / Susanna Foth Aughtmon.
        p.   cm.
    ISBN 978-0-8007-3172-4 (pbk.)
    1. Aughtmon, Susanna Foth, 1970– 2. Christian biography—United States.
    3. Women—Religious life. I. Title.
BR1725.A863A3  2009
248.8′43—dc22                                          2008032507

Scripture is taken from the *Holy Bible*, New Living Translation, copyright © 1996.
Used by permission of Tyndale House Publishers, Inc., Wheaton, Illinois 60189. All
rights reserved.

For my supersisters—Erica, Jenny, Traci, and Chéri

You inspire me. I see Jesus in the ways you love the people around you. May the laughs be endless and the chocolate plentiful as you keep following the One who loves you the most.

# contents

# foreword

The best writers make you feel as though they are your best friend. And I have a feeling you're about to make a new best friend. Susanna Aughtmon is one of the most gifted and likable writers I've ever read. And the truth is, Sue was a friend before I even picked up the book. A few years ago, I had the privilege of doing ministry with Sue and her husband, Scott. They were part of our team at National Community Church in Washington, DC, before they left to plant Pathway Church in Palo Alto, California. It was awfully hard to let them go, because they are some of the nicest and funniest people I know.

While *All I Need Is Jesus and a Good Pair of Jeans* is intended primarily for women, I found it awfully enlightening as a man. In fact, I think husbands should read it before giving it to their wives! How would I describe my experience reading this book? In a word, fun! And that is a supreme compliment. So many books lose me in the second paragraph. But you aren't going to want to put this book down!

Here's what I experienced as I read *All I Need Is Jesus and a Good Pair of Jeans.* It is almost as if Sue walks into a confessional booth and invites us as readers to go in with her. She shares personal struggles that take tremendous courage to reveal. At times, I found myself thinking, *Did she really write that?* But I also found myself identifying with the same struggles. It was so refreshing and encouraging to know that I'm not alone. And I think that is the true reason for confession. It's not just to get something off our shoulders. It's so the hearer, or in this case the reader, knows they aren't alone.

One other warning. You're going to laugh. Hard. Sue has a way of looking at life that will make you laugh and make you think. It will also give you a greater appreciation for the little things we take for granted.

I have a simple theory as a reader and writer: good writers are far less impressive than good people. Sue is both. So without delay, time to go into the confessional booth and begin your own journey toward authentic wholeness.

Mark Batterson
lead pastor, National Community Church,
author, *In a Pit with a Lion on a Snowy Day*

# acknowledgments

Super thanks to . . .

Jesus. Because without him there would be no book.

Scott. I love your care of me, your belief in me, your encouragement. Maybe you made me a little funny. ILUTM.

Jack, Will, and Addison. You are my heart. I could squeeze you forever.

Mom and Dad. You always believed in me. Your love shaped me. I am grateful.

Chris. I love your generous heart. You always make me laugh.

Dave and Lola. For priceless hours of babysitting. You are the best in-laws ever.

Clements, Moodys, Foths, and Bondonnos. You are the best.

Rene. Hilarious friend and writing mentor. This book is as much yours as it is mine. At long last, we did it!

Aly. My writing adventures were inspired by your birth. How fun that I penned my last word while you took care of your cousins. You rock.

Mark and Lora and the NCC crew. We can't get enough of you guys.

And to all of my superfriends. Beth and Gretchen, Barb and Les, the Blakeley cousins, the Pathway crew, the Circus girls, and my Tired Supergirl bloggie friends. My life is better for having you in it.

And for this rich writing experience . . .

My agent, Wendy Lawton. Without your expertise, this book would not have taken flight. I'm grateful for your wit and wisdom.

My editor, Vicki Crumpton. Who got my humor from the start. This process with you has been a treat.

The Revell team and Baker Publishing Group. To each person who laid a hand, prayed a prayer, and immersed themselves in this project, I am eternally grateful.

# introduction

It's always interesting to me to think about my real life versus the life I long for. I am pretty brilliant when it comes to imagining what my life should be. A life without distress. A life with perfect marital communication, obedient children, a clean house, a wealth of friends living on the same block sharing recipes and coffee over the back fence, a thriving growing relationship with Jesus, a conquering of all my weaknesses and struggles, and let's not forget, a good pair of jeans. You know, the type of jeans that give meaning to life. Jeans that suppress the upper thigh, lengthen the inseam, and let you reveal your inner rock star. Because they look that good.

These are a pair of pants that could lead us to believe there is some hope in the world. Hope for a slim leg and a new tomorrow. We tired supergirls tend to call these kind of jeans "forgiving." Because we need some forgiveness when it comes to our jeans. We need something to forgive the saddlebags that hitch up on the side of our legs. Some of us need some forgiveness in the extra girth around our middle. A few of us need some dark-wash forgiveness to camouflage the ripples and bumps hidden therein. Some of us need some forgiveness in flat areas to the rear. We need some lift and extra curves where there are no curves. (I'm not sure who these people are, but I've heard there are some people who need more curves, and I would like to offer up some of mine on their behalf.) And then there are those of us who are deep in over our heads with the fight against cellulite, and nothing aids in this fight, nothing forgives like a nice full coverage denim with some stretch in the fabric. How we love the stretch.

But all of this is to say, some of us have been looking for years for the holy grail of jeans. That pair that will bring to life all that we hope and long to have happen in a pair of jeans. Because we know that there is a standard of what a good pair of jeans is supposed to look like. And then there is the reality of what we look like in our everyday jeans. And we are not wearing grandma-cover-the-belly-button kind of jeans. We have outdone ourselves searching for the most flattering pair of jeans available. We have searched high and low for a good pair of low-rise, easy on the eyes, sturdy on the thighs pair of jeans, and we have bought quite a few pairs, but we are still searching for *the* pair of jeans.

And it's the same when we look at the rest of our lives. What we desire is not necessarily what we have. The person we are is not the person we long to be. Just as the perfect jeans seem to elude us, so do the obedient children, the perfect marital communication, and the conquering of all of our weaknesses. In fact, last time I checked, it seemed like despite all the churchgoing and devotional reading, the weaknesses seemed to be conquering us. So not only have we not found the perfect pair of jeans, but we are still struggling with anxiety and pride and an incapacitating love for chocolate. It seems that we supergirls need some forgiveness in other areas of our lives besides jeans and outerwear. We need forgiveness for our lives in general. And what we really need is some grace. An ever-present shower of grace that we can sit under and soak up and let pervade all the areas of our life that seem to fall short of the glory of God.

We need a whole lot of Jesus. Because there is this woman that we long to be and then there is the woman that we actually are. Right here. Right now. The woman who struggles but longs to be more. The woman who is empty who longs to be full. The dissatisfied woman who longs to be content. The woman who longs to be overflowing with goodness and peace and have her impulse spending under control. And the only thing that can bridge the gap between these two women is buckets of grace. Unending grace. And the only person who embodies this grace is Jesus.

And so the search begins. The search for the woman we were designed to be. The search for some measure of forgiveness as we recognize the person we are and move toward the person we long to become. The search for the One who can infiltrate our lives with his presence, his good sense, and his immeasurable grace that will surely come in handy. It will be quite a journey. That is for sure. But there is always the hope that along the way, we may stumble upon a good pair of jeans.

1

# I AM OH SO TIRED

I am wild-eyed. I have large eyes in general. I'm okay with that. It leaves a lot of room for eye shadow experimentation. It's the wildness that bothers me. It comes from the disparity of life. That space that lives between the expectation of how I thought life would be and the reality of how it is. Like how it hits you unawares that you are over thirty. Or how I can say the words "Put your underwear back on" seven times to my four-year-old in one half-hour period. How getting any semblance of work done requires a cosmic alignment of the planets. Or how I have loved Jesus since age five and still struggle with consistent devotions. How the busyness and anxiety of life choke out its joys and freedoms.

There is this tension between who I want to be and who I really am. Hence the wild big eyes that live in my head.

I called my mom the other day. "I've got to get myself together," I told her.

"Are you still trying that?" she asked.

I really am trying to gather up the pieces of my scattered self . . . on a daily basis. I start out my mornings shooting prayers at the four corners of my bedroom.

"God, I need you."

"God, help me be more like you."

"Please help me get more done."

"Where are my sweats?"

That's not so much a prayer as a request. Which I think God honors. Because of all the prayers, that one usually gets answered the quickest.

But the wildness ensues. It is the mayhem of everyday living that wears me down. I'm a pastor's wife. A mom of three. A housekeeper/organizer/errand runner/etc. A Sunday school teacher. A worship leader. A volunteer at my son's elementary school. On a good day I may squeeze in some exercise or a smattering of writing. And lo and behold, the heavy breathing begins. The chasing after life like a crazy-gaited chicken. And this craziness releases the screaming meemie within when life presses in too hard.

I bark at my children. "Hurry up!"

I nag my husband. "In some countries, people put away clean clothes instead of decorating with them."

I berate myself. "I cannot believe I forgot that appointment . . . again."

I am just a woman. One woman freaking out on a planet full of a lot of other women who, I think, are also freaking out. It's not just the ones with kids. Those of us who have kids are just laid bare more easily because our children know us for who we really are and they tell on us.

My friend Melissa gave me a pair of underwear that says "Supergirl" on the back, as a gag gift. I, however, wear them because new underwear is a novelty, and I'll never turn down a good pair of panties. One morning, my son Jack burst into my room as I was changing clothes and spied the back of my underwear. As I hurriedly hiked up my pants, he gave me a knowing look and said, "Mom, your secret identity has been revealed."

Too late. He knows who I long to be. I really would like to be Supergirl. I would love to leap tall laundry in a single bound. To see through the conundrums of life with X-ray vision or maneuver through the week with energy, compassion, and the extraterrestrial ability to finish my to-do list.

But my super life has gotten the kryptonite smackdown. I have run headlong into my nemesis. She is Tired Lady. She is loathsome and cruel, leaving those in her path lonely and full of self-pity. She zaps me with her Lazy Ray and trips me up with her Rope of Depression, leaving chaos in her wake. I know her well.

My friend Marie France claims that she appears right around 8:30. The children are in bed. A good two or three hours of free time loom before you. Time to clean. Time to think deep thoughts. Time to paint your toenails. Time to snuggle your husband. But Tired Lady sneaks in, crazy gluing your rear to the sofa, leaving your dishes unwashed, your man unsnuggled, your Bible reading undone. It is by no small act of God that you are able to drag yourself off to bed, promising that tomorrow will be a different day. You will vanquish Tired Lady to her Hole of Doom. You'll be the woman God designed you to be. Or at least knock out a load of laundry so your husband doesn't have to turn his underwear inside out anymore. You've got great plans . . . for tomorrow.

I walk the fine line of living between these two identities. I live in the tension of who I want to be and who I really am. It's exhausting, lonely, and wild-eyed.

It reminds me of Peter. He runs willy-nilly through the Gospels, trying to figure out who and where he is supposed to be. Despite Peter's inconsistencies, Jesus sees the space in between who he is and who he could be. He changes his name from Simon to Peter, "The Rock." He is going to be solid.

On the night of the Last Supper, Jesus asks Peter, James, and John to hang out with him. He just wants them to pray with him. Peter is ready to live up to his name. To hunker down and pray like crazy for this man who radically changed his life.

That's when Tired Lady, or maybe in this case, Sleepy Man, creeps in between the fig trees and fern, filling Peter's head with swirly dreams and the inability to process just one tiny prayer. He barely bows his head to pray before the crumbles of wine-dipped bread begin settling in his tummy.

Earlier, Peter had sworn he would never desert the Lord. Jesus tells him that before the rooster crows twice that he will deny him three times. Peter is serious about dying for Jesus. He really believes he is that committed. Or maybe he'll have a nap first and then die for him; it is better to die for someone when you are well rested. Peter's betrayal begins long before the crowing of the bird. It begins with the whiffling snores of deep sleep that break the stillness of Gethsemane. Jesus finds Peter snoozing instead of interceding.

> Then he returned and found the disciples asleep. "Simon!" he said to Peter. "Are you asleep? Couldn't you stay awake and watch with me even one hour? Keep alert and pray. Otherwise temptation will overpower you. For though the spirit is willing enough, the body is weak."
>
> Mark 14:37–38

I wonder if Jesus calls him "Simon" because he just isn't cutting it as "the Rock." Jesus returns to his prayers and Simon goes back to sleep. In all, Jesus wakes him up three times that night. Poor Peter. I have to say that I *love love love* Peter. Like me, he just can't pull it together.

He had visions of being the Rock . . . which I imagine to be a fairly impressive Jewish superhero, comparable to my Supergirl. The Rock was going to rock Israel with his Jesus style, catch a ton of fish, lead a Torah study, bring a few pals to repentance, and squeeze in family time on the weekends, not to mention support Jesus, who simply asked him to stay awake, pray for him, and just be a good buddy the night before he dies a horrible death. And he couldn't do it. And it gets worse after the nap.

> When [Jesus] returned to them the third time, he said, "Still sleeping? Still resting? Enough! The time has come. I, the Son of Man, am betrayed into the hands of sinners. Up, let's be going. See, my betrayer is here!"
>
> Mark 14:41–42

And why is it that during this whole sleepy ordeal, Judas, the betrayer, was wide awake?

Peter goes on to cut off a guard's ear, denies knowing Jesus three times, and deserts him as he hangs on the cross. That is a rough forty-eight-hour ride, from the euphoric heights of the triumphal entry to the crash and burn of Christ's crucifixion. Yep, it definitely gets worse after the nap.

So where does that leave us supergirls? Because we, too, in our heart of hearts long to be all that God created us to be. We are just so darn tired. We are kicked sideways by life, grounded by our expectations, and haunted by our dreams. Will we ever be who we were meant to be?

Well, by the time Acts rolls around, Peter is doing it. He is preaching to multitudes with authority. He has gotten it together. Or maybe, just maybe, he has gotten over himself. Peter could be the Rock because he let God be God.

So, here I am in this space. I am not rocking it. I am barely breathing after kids, work, church, disappointment, and weaknesses cloud my vision. But I have the hope that Peter has. That God knows who I am and who I am supposed to be, and even though I am frequently caught napping, Christ is not done with me.

So maybe I can say this prayer as I ride the edge of imperfection and am caught on the cusp of crazy living.

God, who knows me and keeps me,
Forgive me
Help me get over who I think I am
Help me let go of who I am not
Help me let you be who you are
Don't ever leave me
Amen.

2
# I AM NOT A
# SUPERMODEL

I stand in front of the mirror. Sometimes I am satisfied. Sometimes I am not. Sometimes I would like to wish my thighs into another universe. It's strange, the consuming obsession with looks in our world, because it is just a matter of time before the wrinkles overtake us. We supergirls are in hard-core denial that some day, that stooped lady with polyester pants and orthopedic shoes will be us. We know that beauty is fleeting. But if it is fleeting, we have all donned our track shoes and are racing after it with everything we've got.

We supergirls know how to put on a good show. Our jeans make our legs look longer. Liner makes our lips look fuller. Undergarments make our bodies appear ripple free. My personal favorite is concealer. Baby #2 gifted me with large dark circles under my eyes. Concealer makes me look fresh and dewy eyed, not like the haggard mother of a child who refused to sleep through the night for eight months.

We want to be beautiful. It's a quest that all Western women embark upon at some age or another . . . unless you are a hippy and join a commune. But even then you have to grow out your hair and wear the right ponchos. It just happens. We want to look a certain way. We want to be babelicious.

Beauty truly is in the eye of the beholder. The standard of beauty differs throughout the world. My sister Jenny is a world traveler. She lived in West Africa for four years, working for a relief organization. Her first day on the job, one of her co-workers summed her up with this compliment: "She has a pretty face, a nice smile, and good hips." Beauty equaled curves. They always encouraged Jenny to eat more and be curvier. One male co-worker would greet her daily, saying, "Just five more kilos! Five more kilos!" (Just ten more pounds! Ten more pounds!)

During a stint in Cambodia, Jenny went to get measured for a skirt. The seamstresses could not believe the measurement difference between her hour-glass-shaped waist and hips. One kept saying to the other, "Tuot! Tuot nah!" (Fat! Very fat!)

Which again was a compliment. In Cambodia, most women are rail thin. There is little difference between their waist and hips. Any roundness of shape means that you have money to feed yourself well. The ladies thought Jenny was rich. Jenny was not amused, rich or not.

Our western culture dictates that we should be waif-like. For all of us women who tend to be more Rubenesque, maybe we should jump a plane to West Africa or Cambodia. Not only would we be considered hot, we would be rich. But it's not just our body shape that we are concerned about; it is the whole package. Take hairstyles, for instance.

In the late eighties when big hair was a nationwide phenomenon, my friend Barbie had the most fantastic hair you could imagine. With curly, blonde, voluminous locks that spilled down her back, she rocked a spiral perm like nobody's business. Her high bangs were to die for. Barbie had it goin' on. Her hair was the standard by which I measured my own eighties hair. My hair was light brown and stick straight. It is very difficult to attain big hair when your hair longs to be straight, no matter how many perms you have endured. No matter how high I ratted my bangs and pouffed out the sides of my hair, I could never attain

Barbie's golden-haired glory. And why did I even care anyway? Why couldn't I be satisfied with the baby fine head of hair I was blessed with? That would be because of Nemesis #2. Compare-a-girl.

Compare-a-girl is a nasty one. She has no cellulite and she looks good in spandex. She vaguely resembles that girl in high school who was everything you were not. She constantly reminds you how you will never compare with other supergirls. Compare-a-girl's mindless chatter dribbles on and on like the steady drip of a faucet.

*Drip.* "Look at that girl. Her figure is perfect. If only you could be more like her."

*Drop.* "If only you could lose five pounds and have cheekbones like Frieda."

*Drip.* "It would be nice if you were a little taller like Daphne. You wouldn't look so squatty."

*Drop.* "You wouldn't need that fancy hair product with fifteen proteins and the oil of the rare purple kumquat if your hair was thicker like Sheila's."

*Drip. Drop.* "Why can't you look amazing every day of your life like other people? You'll never measure up."

Rarely do we say these things out loud to ourselves, but the pitter-patter of comparison in our minds leaves us awash in a flood of discontentment. All the magazines, commercials, books, and talk shows we subject ourselves to say that to be admired and powerful, to be loved and happy, we need to be beautiful. I need to be beautiful . . . like _____. (Fill in the name of your favorite celebrity or prettiest co-worker.)

A lot of my happiness seems to be based on how I stack up against the next girl. Guys seem to be a little more balanced in this area. I have never seen my husband look at a magazine cover and say, "Why can't I look like him? . . . I wonder what hair product he uses to get that natural wave?"

That would be disturbing. But . . . I think things like that.

In a magazine interview, Rachel Hunter, the supermodel, said she eats healthily, exercises, and has a great life, but there are still a few things she would like to change about herself. Who is she comparing *herself* to? Let's just say that Compare-a-girl has inspired a lot of cosmetic surgery. One sixty-five-year-old lady in New York keeps trying to get her eyes to look like they did when she was twenty-three. She now has her eyebrows pulled back to her ears. It's not pretty.

I color my hair. I use teeth-whitening toothpaste. When I have a few minutes, I pluck my eyebrows. Due to my Eastern European descent, I have three sets: the ones that grow over my eyebrows, the ones that grow under my eyebrows, and my actual eyebrows. I try to look put together. I'm beginning to moisturize. I do a bit of stretching. I don lip gloss.

I go for the "cool young mom, hey, I run after three little boys all day" look. My sister Erica throws the "I'm hip and my teenage daughter's friends are impressed with my style" look. My sister Jenny hits it with the "I'm classy, sassy, and I wear Italian leather pointy boots" look. The pointy boot look would not work for me, as I am often knee-deep in sand or clinging to play structures and would impale small children on them while going down the slide. At the core, we three supersisters are saying the same thing. I want to be beautiful. I want to be admired. I want to be loved.

The quest for beauty is a timeless issue. I bet Eve thought, *I was so much hotter before I sinned and got kicked out of the garden.* The apostle Paul actually addressed the women in the church regarding their style, saying,

And I want women to be modest in their appearance. They should wear decent and appropriate clothing and not draw attention to themselves by the way they fix their hair or by wearing gold or pearls or expensive clothes. For women who claim to be devoted to God should make themselves attractive by the good things they do.

1 Timothy 2:9–10

How funny is that? Funny, because in two thousand years, we have not changed. I like to think there were some women in that church sporting gold-laced beehives and hot pink togas. And I think a few of them were probably catty.

"Did you see her sandals? They are so 28 BC."

Or, "Bless her heart, doesn't she know they only wear their hair like that in Athens? Let's pray for her."

When I'm feeling a bit insecure, I tend to notice and celebrate the imperfections of others. It draws attention away from my own inadequacies. Compare-a-girl likes to work it that way too. If you are feeling bad about yourself, she'll encourage you to find someone who looks a little worse off than you and point out all their flaws. She's a winner all the way around.

I don't think Paul is saying you need to be a plain Jane. We were made to enjoy beauty. God values beauty. He created us to enjoy the loveliness, the magnificence of his creation, people included. I think Paul is reminding these women to refocus their attention on real beauty.

Real beauty is not so much how we look but who we are. We were created in God's image, to reflect his glory. What we supergirls really want is not to be America's next top model but to be women who attract people to Jesus. The image we portray draws attention to ourselves. The way we act, the way we love, the attitudes we embrace, have the ability to draw attention to God. And while there is nothing wrong with taking care of our appearance, our ultimate goal is to use our lives to point others toward Christ. That is what Paul is reminding us of.

Those words of comfort, the grace and mercy we pour out, the acceptance of any person regardless of hairstyle, is so beautiful. So attractive. The way we love Jesus and do things that we wouldn't normally do, like forgive our enemies and share our chocolate, that is true beauty, and people are drawn to it. Then by some amazing, breathtaking miracle, they see Jesus in us and are drawn to him. They are drawn to God, the designer of the universe, because we are lovely on the inside.

If we can figure out a way to get beyond our own need to be physically beautiful and focus on who God is, what he has done for us, and the grace that he has lavished on us, we can learn about being content. Contentment. It's the weapon that takes Compare-a-girl out at the knees. She rushes in to backhand you with your lack of style, and you say, "Aha!" Block! Kick! Crunch! "Did you forget, Compare-a-girl, oh evil spandex-loving one, that God loves me and I'm good with my eighties hair?" Body block! High kick! Karate chop!

"Aaaaaargh! I'm sinking into the abyss of contentedness!" she shrieks.

Good riddance. Paul knew that he could be content with little or much because his focus wasn't on what he had or how he looked or even who he was. His focus, his life, was about pointing others Christ-ward. Using his life to reflect God's glory. And even us supergirls, whether we are just entering the beauty race, rounding the last bend, or hanging up our track shoes and donning our orthopedic footwear, can still do that. Because in all his mercy and forgiveness, in his all-encompassing love of us, Christ is the most lovely. When we soak up who Christ is, when we emulate his love and grace and reflect his glory, we, too, are truly beautiful. Take that, Compare-a-girl. Hi-yah!

3
# I HAVE PRIDE ISSUES

With all of my faults, my weaknesses, my craziness, my low self-esteem, you would think that I wouldn't have a lot of room for pride. That's what you would think. But surprisingly, it flourishes, with great abundance. At least it did . . . until this year. Shall we call it the year of humbling?

The problem is that pride comes so naturally to us supergirls. Pride is simply this: I am better than you. We know how good it feels to be better than someone else. Our whole culture revolves around pride. Superstars! Business moguls! Power geeks! Who doesn't want to be number one?

Back to my humbling. I vaguely recall hearing the phrase "Pride goes before a fall."

My problem was that I was oblivious to how prideful I was. I've never thought of myself in those terms. But I do like to be right. I don't want people to teach me. I don't like to fail, so if I'm not good at something, I avoid it. Meet Mrs. Prideful. She wreaks havoc in the lives of unsuspecting supergirls. The problem is that we don't recognize how powerful she is. She hangs onto the backs of our earrings and whispers lies in our ears.

"You've got this one. Don't ask for help. You can do it on your own."

Or . . . "Hmm . . . I'm not really sure if you should hang out with her . . . I've heard that she is needy. You should be around people who are healthy and wholesome . . . like yourself."

Lucky for us, we supergirls are pretty capable of handling anything thrown our way. We just avoid doing anything that exposes our weaknesses. And we know how to get around problem people. Since Jesus wants us to be loving, we'll be extra nice but aloof. We don't want to get involved with anyone who's too messy. If these needy people could reach our level of maturity, then we would love to have coffee, but until then, "Buh-bye!"

I'm pretty sure that I have just described a Pharisee . . . you know, one of those religious guys that Jesus called sweet names like, "Oh you brood of vipers." This loosely translated means: "Oh you big group of really poisonous snakes."

What is more obnoxious than a nice aloof person who thinks she is better than you? We have all met her; we just didn't realize we were her. Supergirl alert! Pride is sneaky and mean. (Footnote: you aren't better than anyone else.)

Oh, the pain of it. But back to my humbling. Did I mention that this year has been downright ugly? In January, my husband and I started a church plant in Palo Alto, California, near Stanford University, which could be the birthplace of pride. It is full of pretty, smart, number-one kind of people who go off to do small things like invent Yahoo and run countries, which seems to add to the irony of my situation.

We were aching to get at this thing and do it right. Mostly, Scott was aching and I was terrified—in an aching kind of way. Pastoring is his passion. But church planting calls for all to be involved. We all wear many hats. One of my jobs is to lead worship. I have always sung backup, but leading worship, I think, is a calling. For a person who reveres the appearance of being in control, there was a general uprising by Mrs. Prideful.

I believe "Heavenly daystars, no!" was her outcry.

I like to be calm. And comfortable. I prefer accolades to pity. I would rather have someone think that I have it all together than realize I am falling apart. I like to keep up appearances.

For four consecutive months, I experienced nausea, diarrhea, and intense anxiety every Sunday morning. I couldn't think of things to say in between songs. My voice shook. Sometimes I cried, usually before the service, so I was nice and splotchy for worship time. Let me weave you some woeful tales of worship leading.

There was the Sunday when we didn't have childcare and I tried to hold my eighteen-month-old while leading worship. The body bends, the arching of the back, and the general screaming of Will led no one into God's presence.

Then there was the Sunday a bunch of Stanford students visited. The entire first song was accompanied by a high-pitched screeching from our monitors. Not one of them has returned.

Then there was Memorial Day Sunday. We sang for fifteen minutes. With no one there. Except Jesus. I'm hoping he liked it, because it felt a bit awkward to me.

The crowning glory of humblings was the singing of "It Is Well with My Soul." I told our group the story behind the hymn.

The hymn writer loses his only son to scarlet fever, then his financial holdings in the Great Chicago fire. His wife and four daughters sail to England for a respite, and the ship goes down. Only his wife survives. As he sails to join his grief-stricken wife, the captain calls him up to the bridge to show him where his daughters' ship went down. He returns to his cabin and writes "It Is Well with My Soul."

As I finished the story, we were all moved, ready to sing this anthem to God. Lo and behold, I couldn't find the note to start the song. Three times, I started to lead the congregation in a hideous off-key rendition of "It Is Well with My Soul." I was about to throw myself to the ground in shame when Anthony, on guitar, hummed the note in my ear. God bless him! We went on to sing the full hymn, somewhat haphazardly. I recall Mrs. Prideful fleeing the building in hysterics.

These are just a few examples of how God has led me down the "get over yourself" path, through the valley of "I've fallen and I can't get up," toward the "I need you like never before" mountains. I think that God takes pride very seriously, because when we are full of ourselves, there is no room left for him to occupy.

Pride lets you lie to yourself about who you are. Being full of pride, I could tell myself I have it together. I can lead worship. I don't need to ask for help or to be taught. Glen, a campus ministry leader at Stanford, gave a talk at our church about humility around the same time I was grappling with all my worship woes. One of his points really stuck with me: humility lets you recognize yourself for who you are. In my case, humility meant saying I am scared. I don't know how to do this. There are people who do this better than I do. I need God to fill me up because I can't possibly do it on my own.

Jesus was so over people who pretended they had it all together. Every time he would come up against pride, he would squash it. He was the Savior of the world, and he was the most humble. In humility, he recognized himself for who he truly was. Emmanuel. God with us. The most accepting. The most loving. He hung out with losers. Fishermen and tax collectors, left-wing zealots and shifty-eyed sellouts. He forgave prostitutes. He partied with the masses. And the prideful, the law keepers, the Pharisees, he drove them nuts.

He defied their control, their careful wording of questions, their rules and regulations with jokes and wittiness and love. The real people, the ones with their problems written on their faces and their sins flung out in the open, they adored him. Because they knew he was on their side.

I don't think that God is into humiliating people. He gives us gifts and wants us to use them for his glory and purposes. But I do think that he wants us to recognize ourselves for who we really are. We are scared, imperfect people who desperately need him to fill our lives with his truth and clarity. We need the ability to accept ourselves and others without reservation, like he does. He never said, "Come unto me all you who are smart, who had time to work out, who know a bazillion Scriptures, and have all the problems of the universe solved. I'm prideful and I have a lot of expectations. I am perfect. Be like me. In general, you will be exhausted every day trying to live up to my example."

It goes something like this:

Then Jesus said, "Come to me, all of you who are weary and carry heavy burdens, and I will give you rest. Take my yoke upon you. Let me teach you, because I am humble and gentle, and you will find rest for your souls. For my yoke fits perfectly, and the burden I give you is light."

Matthew 11:28–30

I never got that from Mrs. Prideful. I could never live up to the person she told me I should be.

Are you tired? Are you weighed down with the heaviness of life? Jesus wants to team up with you. The yoke he wants you to share is light, and if we let him, he carries most of the load. Because he can. He's God. If we lean into him, knowing who we really are, in all our weakness, he will provide for us and care for us and teach us, because he knows who he really is. The Almighty. And how about some rest? He'd like to give you a break. We get to leave the trying and the pretending of being prideful and embrace the easiness of humility when we attach ourselves to Christ.

And now that Mrs. Prideful has been ripped from our earrings and been banished to her prideful lair, I think we will actually be able to hear what Jesus is whispering in our ears. That he loves us. Just as we are.

# 4
# I WORRY
# ABOUT THINGS

I worry. A lot. I have some anxiety. I've been known to be filled with angst. I worry about our finances. All the time. I worry about my family. I worry about my friends and their struggles. I worry about pollution, wars, and conflict in the world. I worry about our church and the success of our ministry along with the fact that my house is never clean and the laundry never ends. I worry about people who don't know Jesus and about the people who do know Jesus but don't act like him. I worry about the strip of spider veins that wrapped itself around my upper thigh when I wasn't looking.

Worry is an endless, vicious cycle. It is a game played in the mind, and we supergirls never win. There is always something to worry about. There are many, many things that are stressful and wrong in this world. It is, quite literally, all going to hell in a handbasket. Everywhere you turn there is some sort of conflict or crisis on a global level. If we take it down to tired supergirl level, the world that we live in and where we try to walk out our journey of faith, we are constantly hit by a barrage of inconsistencies, trials, and general mayhem. Relationships going awry. Stressful work situations. Financial burdens. Physical ailments. Plumbing issues. Fashion disasters. Church spats. It makes a supergirl tired just thinking about it. And that is what we do. Think. Ponder. Agonize.

Thanks to our good friend Worry Man. Here he comes to wreck the day! Worry Man likes to remind us of things we should be using our brain power on and focusing our emotional energy toward. Anything we can worry about, he will bring up. There you are, minding your own business, gingerly sipping on a latte, and BAM!

"I don't think your mom likes your boyfriend. You better think about that."

Or, "I wonder why your best friend didn't call you this past weekend? I wonder if she's hanging out with someone else. Huh."

He likes to frame his thoughts with phrases like "You should be concerned about . . ." or "Have you ever wondered about . . ."

That's all it takes to set our minds off into a frenzy of "what ifs" and "I thinks" as we create false conversations in our head and imagine different scenarios of how these situations will play out. Worry Man is trying to impress upon us that we have the power to change something with our worrying.

The other day, I was late getting back to my house. I was supposed to be at home baking scones and prepping coffee for the playgroup I had offered to host. Two other moms were coming. I was already a bit harried that I hadn't swept the kitchen floor or picked up the toys littering our living room. At the time my friends Paula and Angie were supposedly arriving at my house, I was still fifteen minutes away from home. My mind began to race with all the things these two friends must be thinking of me, like how inconsiderate I was to invite them over and not be home when they arrived. Or how they would look with disdain upon my unkempt, crumb-covered carpet. Or how utterly disgusted they would be to find out there were no scones of any kind, not even a baggy of stale graham crackers waiting for them, when they were welcomed into my home.

This thought process escalated in my mind to an impending altercation.

I imagined Paula and Angie berating me for my thoughtlessness. I imagined how I would have to defend my actions, my dirty house, and lack of breakfast goods, maybe using some form of karate and the Jedi mind trick to get them to see how I hadn't set out to intentionally ruin their morning. Mind you, both Paula and Angie are the most laid-back, gracious women you will ever meet. We laugh a lot when we are together and have never come to blows over a lack of pastry. I have never seen either one angry, let alone throw down over a late playdate. But that is beside the point.

Worry Man was working overtime in this tired supergirl's head. He had me on the mat, pinned down by anxiety and frustration, and I was worn out by the time I pulled up into my driveway. Angie was standing by her car, holding her four-week-old infant. I jumped out, feeling a bit defensive and, above all things, worried.

"How long have you been waiting? I am so sorry," I burbled on until she said, "Oh, I just got here." At that moment my phone rang.

I answered to find out Paula was just leaving her house and wouldn't be getting there for another fifteen minutes. It was all I could do to keep from collapsing on the couch utterly exhausted and emotionally wrung out. And all for no reason. No reason! They were both running late too, and seemed remarkably at ease with themselves, while I had been caught up in an emotional quagmire with Worry Man, rehearsing different angry scenarios in my head.

And so we come to the futility of worrying that Jesus addressed on the Sermon on the Mount. He talked to the crowd in a way they had never heard before. He talked about real-life stuff, not heady theology.

So I tell you, don't worry about everyday life—whether you have enough food, drink, and clothes. Doesn't life consist of more than food and clothing? Look at the birds. They don't need to plant or harvest or put food in barns because your heavenly Father feeds them. And you are far more valuable to him than they are. Can all your worries add a single moment to your life? Of course not.

Matthew 6:25–27

(And yet, worry comes so very naturally. We supergirls think worrying about things may add at least a little clarity to our lives. And we're not really worrying . . . we like to call it critical thinking . . . or problem solving . . . after all, we are intelligent people.) Jesus continues:

And why worry about your clothes? Look at the lilies and how they grow. They don't work or make their clothing, yet Solomon in all his glory was not dressed as beautifully as they are. And if God cares so wonderfully for flowers that are here today and gone tomorrow, won't he more surely care for you? You have so little faith!

Matthew 6:28–30

(But did Solomon have to worry about a good pair of jeans? We're not sure how it all went down back then, but jeans are the staple our fashion life hinges on. They are far past utilitarian. We can dress them up. We can dress them down. Finding the right wash, fit, and style is enough to cause even the most worthy of us supergirls to worry.)

So don't worry about having enough food or drink or clothing. Why be like the pagans who are so deeply concerned about these things? Your heavenly Father already knows all your needs, and he will give you all you need from day to day if you live for him and make the Kingdom of God your primary concern. So don't worry about tomorrow, for tomorrow will bring its own worries. Today's trouble is enough for today.

Matthew 6:31–34

Now that whole pagan comment. That's a little bit hurtful. It suggests that the people who were supposed to be following God were caught up in the same worries as the people who were not following God, and here Jesus points it out. He asks, "Why?" Because they should have known that if they were following God with all their hearts, he would give them all that they needed. How is it that they got so caught up in the emotional struggle of worrying? Of losing precious thinking time and emotional energy on things they had absolutely no control over? Their worry would not change that. Now you would think that Jesus was speaking directly to a bunch of supergirls in this passage. Because here is where Jesus gets at the heart of the worrying issue.

Sometimes we supergirls think that God is not concerned with the details of our lives. We know that he cares about the condition of our hearts or any variety of heavenly issues. But when it comes to our daily living, like paying the rent or finding a good job or that last guy we dated, not to mention the right pair of jeans, that is something that doesn't really concern God and we need to take care of that ourselves. But that is the exact opposite of what Jesus says. He strips it down to the most basic of necessities. What will you eat, drink, or wear today? Don't run after it. God has already taken care of it. Just seek him, and everything else will be given to you.

While we are focusing all our thoughts on fixing problems, imagining outcomes, and replaying conversations that have already taken place, we could be communicating with the one who actually has the ability to make a difference in our lives. Jesus is telling us that what we need, God will provide.

Worry Man loses his superpowers when we run after God. It is that simple. Because when we worry (seeking answers in ourselves), we end up where we started. With ourselves. But when we look to God (seeking answers in the creator of the universe), we find an endless supply of answers, miracles, and wisdom that we cannot access any other way. Worry Man says, "Wait, come back, let's think about next week and all the problems that are facing you."

And you say, "I have heard that God even cares about tiny birds, and he meets all their needs, so I think I'll hang out with him and let him take care of next week."

And the beauty of it, tired supergirl, is that he will. It may look different than the outcome you imagined in your head. In fact, it probably will blow you away. That's just how he likes to work things. And just in case you are wondering, he even takes care of playdates that have gone awry. So there, take that, Worry Man.

## 5

# I FORGET THERE IS NO MORE CONDEMNATION IN CHRIST

Rene and I were chatting last night. She is another supergirl trying to keep it real and follow Jesus. We were talking about grace . . . which we would like to have. And peace . . . which we know we should have truckloads of. And freedom from condemnation . . . because that would just make life a lot more pleasant. We would really, really like to get rid of all that condemnation. But we just can't let ourselves. We grew up in church, we know the rules, and we are just too good at knowing how bad we are.

Condemnation. It's all about justice and getting what we deserve. Condemnation is about death. We sin. And the penalty for sin is death. But we're not talking about early Bible times, with the-whole-tribe-of-Israel-knows-your-sin-and-takes-you-outside-of-the-city-walls-and-stones-you condemnation. This is the twenty-first century, for goodness' sake. We're talking about mind-numbing-if-you-only-knew-me-and-what-I've-done-and-how-I-fail-every-day condemnation, where we die small deaths all day long because we know we will never live up to the perfection of Christ.

"I don't need other people to condemn me," Rene reminded me. "I do a really good job of that myself."

That's how it is for a lot of us supergirls. Who needs other people to point out your faults when you do such a good job of it yourself? It slaps you upside the head when you wake up in the morning and runs laps around you when you try to rest at night. You're not good enough. You fail. You sin . . . a lot. You won't ever be who you want to be. Just in case you were wondering, that slapping sensation comes from Condemno Boy, who is lobbing stones at you from the sidelines. His throwing power comes from his unbelievable ability to recall your every shortcoming. All of your less-than moments. Your failures. Your mishaps. Your tales of how you have wronged others. Your great mind-numbing gaffs. Your weak, embarrassing, can't-get-free stories. He throws them back in your face with fantastic speed. Just when you think you are out of his line of fire, just when you start to feel a little grace heading your way, a little mercy freeing up some space in your soul . . . WHAM!

"August 23, 1997 . . . remember how you lied to your boss?"

Then POW!

"November 14, 2004 . . . you went a little too far with boyfriend #3."

Now you're down for the count, and here comes his curve-ball with stunning accuracy . . . ZING!

"This morning, you yelled at your husband, ignored your kids, and ate five chocolate chip cookies for breakfast. Anger, apathy, and gluttony! What a terrific way to start your day. Some Christ follower you are."

And you are speechless. Because he is right.

Condemno Boy smirks . . . victorious once again. He always wins because he is always right. We supergirls are far from perfect. Even though we know Jesus saved us, we get stuck. Stuck in our sin, our past, our yuckiness.

The thing is . . . sometimes it's hard to get free. We know in our heads that there is absolute freedom in Christ. But really, what does free look like? And what does free feel like?

I know what condemnation looks like. It looks like a broken woman, wrapped in a robe, being carried through the streets. She is sobbing and embarrassed. The Pharisees found her, naked, amidst her sin, and she knows she is going to die. That's what happens when you are caught, mid-adultery, in Jesus's day. You get to die a painful, public death by stoning. Somehow, these men knew where she was and what she was doing, and they are going to take her and Jesus out in one fell swoop. Shame contorts her face as they bring her to him. The Pharisees, good pals of our friend Condemno Boy, trapped her and now they want to see if they can trap Jesus. She is an adulteress . . . what is he going to do about it? It plays out like this:

> They kept demanding an answer, so he stood up again and said, "All right, stone her. But let those who have never sinned throw the first stones!" Then he stooped down again and wrote in the dust.
>
> When the accusers heard this, they slipped away one by one, beginning with the oldest, until only Jesus was left in the middle of the crowd with the woman. Then Jesus stood up again and said to her, "Where are your accusers? Didn't even one of them condemn you?"
>
> "No, Lord," she said.
>
> And Jesus said, "Neither do I. Go and sin no more."
>
> John 8:7–11

And that's that. The Pharisees leave. They can't stone her because they aren't perfect either. Not one of us supergirls is perfect or ever will be. But Jesus is. He is the one who knows our junk, all the ugly stuff. And Jesus, the perfect one, doesn't condemn us. He doesn't excuse our behavior. In fact, he tells the woman, "Go and sin no more." But I think that could only happen once she encountered Jesus. She could only leave behind who she was, the condemnation of what she had done, her sentence of death, after she came face-to-face with Jesus and he set her free. Free. Really free.

48

Paul puts it like this in Romans:

So now there is no condemnation for those who belong to Christ Jesus. For the power of the life-giving Spirit has freed you through Christ Jesus from the power of sin that leads to death.

8:1–2

Paul should know. He met Jesus on a lonely road and was never the same again. He got free.

I think free feels like your first breath of air after being told you are not going to die. I think it feels like the morning after a really hard rain. It's a new start. A breaking free from what we were and running toward who we will be. I think free feels like waves of grace and mercy crashing over us and washing away the mud of the past that weighs down our hearts and buries our souls. I think free looks like a broken woman in a robe who has seen the Messiah and will never be the same again. She was being dragged toward her death and meets life on the way. Free looks like the smile that lights her face as she cuts through the crowd, hurrying toward her new life. Free looks like the stones scattered in the dust, the ones that were never thrown. Free looks like the backs of the accusers as they slip away, one by one.

I think free looks like Jesus, the compassion in his eyes and the stoop of his shoulders as he bends down to write in the dust. Because he doesn't condemn us. Even though we are sinful and the penalty for sin is death. He loves us too much. He couldn't stand for us to die. So he did it himself. And because of that, we get to feel and smell and hear and taste his freedom. The freedom that we supergirls long for. The freedom of fresh starts and new mercies every morning. The freedom that comes from knowing that when we are standing with Jesus, no one gets to throw any stones.

49

6

# I WANT CHOCOLATE TO SOLVE MY PROBLEMS

There is nothing like chocolate. Especially a piece of rich, dark chocolate broken off from a big fat bar. You truly have to savor each bite. Because it will soon be gone. I know this because I am a connoisseur of chocolate. It is an integral part of my existence.

Chocolate is a legacy in my family. My mom, Ruth, would sneak candy bars to make it through the day with four kids under the age of seven. Her mom, Opal, measured her sadness with Hershey almond bars. After Grandpa died, she ate chocolate bars to stave off the pain. Sometimes it was an eight-bar day. Opal's mom, Minnie, loved chocolate too. One young man came courting with a box of chocolates, promising to have her home by curfew. When he returned her home late, she took the box and threw it in the fire. She must have really wanted to be on time because chocolate is precious, like brown gold.

Studies have shown that chocolate can release chemicals in the brain similar to those of being in love. One study shows that pregnant women who eat chocolate are happier and have happier babies. I know this because I ate chocolate while I was pregnant and I was happy. Baby #3, who could be very serene, did flips like a dolphin when it hit his bloodstream. Chocolate is good.

Chocolate is also comforting. When life feels crazy, I know that a brownie can soothe me. Or when the bills come, I reach for anything remotely chocolaty . . . even a chalky protein bar. I, too, gage my grief by the amount of chocolate inhaled. I assuage my anger, my anxiety, and my loneliness with chocolate. The reason? Because if I am eating chocolate, I can focus on the pleasure of the moment and escape from whatever angst is at hand. My name is Susanna, and I am an emotional chocoholic.

By now, you probably pity me for the cocoa-loving freak that I am. Let me introduce you to Mr. Substitution. He keeps me in steady supply. He specializes in plying supergirls with whatever they use to keep their minds off whatever troubles them. He has a wide variety of diversions to offer us supergirls, such as food, relationships, shopping sprees, sex, exercise, knitting, archeology, sunbathing, alcohol, scrapbooking, spa treatments, movies, church functions, cross-country skiing, swing dancing, the office—you name it, he's got it. We all have our drug of choice. And he has cornered the market on chocolate.

Mr. Substitution is pleasant, always helping us supergirls get our minds off of things. He's not against plying supergirls with different options. If you can no longer button your jeans, why not buy some new pants? Your job is holding you hostage? Why not plan a trip to Honolulu? That nice Christian guy you are pining for hasn't made eye contact? Why not go out one last time with your selfish, cheating ex-boyfriend? At least he calls.

Of course, Mr. Substitution is always in hiding whenever you discover the newest patch of cellulite your latest chocolate binge has produced. He is also unavailable whenever the credit card bill arrives. Or when you are hung over after the big soiree he encouraged you to go to. Or drowning in the emotional ravages of another failed relationship he lured you into. He's always absent when you ask God for forgiveness or feel haunted by your weakness. He's on hiatus when you try to search for your answers in God's grace.

Mr. Substitution is tricky. He can never truly alleviate the crushing emptiness within us supergirls. He can only offer us cheap filler. He looks at a hard situation and offers us easy, do-it-yourself solutions. Need comfort? Here's some ice cream. Want love? Have a noncommitted make-out buddy whenever you're lonely. Long for acceptance? Wear the latest styles and watch people gaze at you enviously. Wish for peace? Go to a yoga class and stretch to your heart's content.

The tricky part is that these things we long for are God-given desires. Who doesn't need comfort, love, acceptance, and peace? And usually the substitutions, in and of themselves, aren't bad. Food, intimacy, clothes, and exercise are all good. Here's the catch: Mr. Substitution analyzes our desires and offers us . . . less. Less than what we need. Less than what we long for. Less than what we deserve as supergirls, yearning to follow the Savior of the universe. He offers a quick fix to a lifelong struggle. And we take the fix, over and over, because it's easy. But let's face it, it never lasts.

The chocolate bar ends. The clothes go out of style. The thrill of winning passes. The good-night kiss lingers only so long. The knit one, purl two afghan is finished. The appletini buzz never lasts. And then what? Why, hello, Mr. Substitution! Fancy meeting you here again.

It is like the Samaritan woman Jesus meets at the well. She has this need inside of her that she believes only a man can fill. So she tried one. And then two. And then five. After all, marriage is hard to get right. She longs for intimacy. She eats, breathes, and sleeps it. And inside she's dying, because she can't find this guy. The one. The one who knows her, meets her every need, fills the desire, and makes her feel whole. There is always something missing. Luckily, Mr. Substitution is on hand. She'll make the rounds of the whole town if he has his way.

That is, until she meets the Man. It is a hot day. The streets are dusty, and she can taste the dust on her teeth. The rest of the town is inside waiting out the heat. She makes her way to the well, maybe because she knows no one will be there to turn away from her or look at her with disgust. But he is there. And he doesn't turn away. And when he speaks, grace floods over her. He asks her to get a drink for him, but really he has come to quench her unquenchable thirst. He looks into the well, eyeing the water.

> Jesus replied, "People soon become thirsty again after drinking this water. But the water I give them takes away thirst altogether. It becomes a perpetual spring within them, giving them eternal life."
>
> "Please, sir," the woman said, "give me some of that water! Then I'll never be thirsty again, and I won't have to come here to haul water."
>
> John 4:13–15

(Just think. If she doesn't have to go to the well, she can avoid the rejection of the townspeople who know how she lives.)

> "Go and get your husband," Jesus told her.
>
> "I don't have a husband," the woman replied.
>
> Jesus said, "You're right! You don't have a husband—for you have had five husbands, and you aren't even married to the man you're living with now."
>
> John 4:16–18

Jesus lays it out for her. He knows her inside and out. Her weakness. Her desire. Her scandal. Her deep unmet need. And he is still talking with her. Acknowledging her. Not running from her. "Sir," the woman said, "you must be a prophet" (John 4:19).

Jesus goes on to explain. Not a prophet. Not a man. Not a Jew. Not a teacher. He reveals himself to her. He is the Messiah. The Savior. And he would just like to sit here with her and chat. He rocks her world. A surge of hope fills her. In that moment, she has an epiphany. A taste of God. A kernel of truth pierces her soul. He is the one. This man is the man she's been looking for all of her life. All that searching, the quest for intimacy, the longing for real relationship—it ends here. And it isn't about sex or another marriage or another failed affair; it is about the Christ. He's come to quench her thirst.

All of the sudden, she is swept away by this revelation and she is running. Because she is full. For the first time in her life, she is full to running over. The Bible says,

> The woman left her water jar beside the well and went back to the village and told everyone, "Come and meet a man who told me everything I ever did! Can this be the Messiah?" So the people came streaming from the village to see him.

> John 4:28–30

So this Samaritan woman, who once avoided everyone, races back to her village, yelling, banging on doors, clutching at people, looking them in the eye, and telling them the good news. Her testimony alone sparks a revival in her town. She is changed. Imagine it. I wonder if guy #6 is sent packing. Mr. Substitution can't cut it anymore. She has tasted the real thing. She has spent time with God. He knows her mess. And he still wants to hang out with her. He likes her.

And so it is with us supergirls and our quiet longings and empty substitutions. He knows our mess. He knows about the crying and aching and the longing to be full. He knows about the shopping and the overtime at work, the romance novels and the trips to Baskin Robbins. And he still wants to hang out. He really likes us. If we drink in his forgiveness and mercy, we don't have to be thirsty anymore. We've invited him to come in and change our world before, but let's do it again. It's just one more trip to the well, but this is no ordinary drink.

I can't get the chorus to this Bethany Dillon song out of my head. It talks about how Jesus can take a regular day and make it new. That when he enters the picture, everything changes. He sees our hurt and suffering and weeps over it and begins to fashion us into a new person. It's a praise song. The kind of praise song a supergirl would sing after chatting with God. Instead of eating a bar of chocolate.

**7**
# I SIN A LOT

The word *sin* is just so ugly. If I had my choice, I'd rather think about things like Hawaii and buy-one-get-one-free sales. Sin conjures up thoughts of imperfection and wrongdoing. I would rather not dwell on such unpleasantness. I like to think about all the things that I get right. All three and a half of them. I feel very comfortable sharing the non-sinful areas of myself with others. Letting people in on my weaknesses makes me feel vulnerable and weird because they might try to hold me accountable or something. I also like to pretend that other people think I don't have any sins. Now my family and friends, they know I have a lot of sin, so I can't pull that one over on them, but I think there are some people in China who think I am sinless. And that makes me feel better about myself.

On the whole, I do pretty good with the Ten Commandments. I have never murdered anyone, and I honor my parents. But it starts getting tricky in the New Testament when Jesus says the two greatest commandments are to love God with all your heart, mind, and strength and to love your neighbor as yourself. That is so all-encompassing. Loving God with all my strength? I need some of my strength for loving chocolate and shopping. And I don't know about you, but some of my "neighbors," the people who surround me in life, are not a bit like me, so how can I be expected to love them like I love myself? Sin has been compared to "missing the mark," an archery term.

If loving God with all my being and loving my neighbor as myself is the bull's-eye, I tend to miss the mark on a spectacularly regular basis.

I'm not sure how I became aware of all the sin in my life, but the craziest thing is the more I move toward God, the more I am in his presence, the more aware I am of how sinful I am. When God is near, I suddenly realize, "Well, for goodness' sake, I've got a whole lot of sins inside of me."

And then I want to hunker down and hide behind something, because it is painful to be sinful when God is right there all perfect and holy.

I take after my predecessors Adam and Eve on that fateful day in the Garden of Eden. They polish off the apple and suddenly start looking for some way to cover up what they have just done. They try wearing some leaves, but when God comes strolling through the garden they realize, "Hey, these leaves are just not big enough to cover our shame! Where is that big juniper bush?"

And sadly enough, evergreen foliage does no better at hiding sin. God has X-ray vision and tends to see through whatever we are hiding behind, taking in the condition of our hearts. The funny thing is, while we know that Adam and Eve got caught, we supergirls think we can hide better. After all, they were pretty lame with their fig leaves. It is a time-honored tradition among tired supergirls to do something wrong . . . hide it . . . pretend it's not there . . . and hope that God doesn't call us out from the bushes exposing us for who we are . . . sinners.

Duck and cover is the brilliant plan of the In-sin-erator. He wants to keep us on the run and in hiding. He knows that as long as there is sin in our hearts, we are separated from God. Of course, he doesn't put it to us this way because none of us wants to be separated from God. So he says things like, "Don't worry. What you did isn't a big deal. If you talk about it now, it will just mess everything up. Just bury it and move on."

Or, "Hey, who says that it's sin anyway? It's a personal choice. You did it to better yourself. Who can argue with that?"

He often recruits Mrs. Prideful to help him out. She likes to remind you, "You don't want to humiliate yourself, do you? Whatever you do, just don't tell anyone what you did. They'll judge you. Think less of you. And they will tell other people about your sin."

The problem with the In-sin-erator's "bury it and move on" plan is that we can't. Once we have buried it, we are stuck in the clutches of whatever it is that we have done. Instead of admitting we made a mistake, we give this mistake the power to keep us hiding and separated from God. If we can't admit to what we have done, we become a slave to it. To the power of the sin. To the fear that we will be found out. To the knowledge that we are imperfect. It's dark and it's ugly, girls, I'm not going to lie. The In-sin-erator wants to keep us in the dark, but Jesus has a different idea.

The apostle John talks about it this way.

This is the message he has given us to announce to you: God is light and there is no darkness in him at all. So we are lying if we say we have fellowship with God but go on living in spiritual darkness. We are not living in the truth. But if we are living in the light of God's presence, just as Christ is, then we have fellowship with each other, and the blood of Jesus, his Son, cleanses us from every sin.

If we say we have no sin, we are only fooling ourselves and refusing to accept the truth. But if we confess our sins to him, he is faithful and just to forgive us and to cleanse us from every wrong. If we claim we have not sinned, we are calling God a liar and showing that his word has no place in our hearts.

1 John 1:5–10

As we tired supergirls are trying to unravel the mysteries of our hearts and all the issues that plague us, we must have a long, soulful chat about sin. Let's call it what it is. We might as well shout it from the mountaintops. *We have a lot of sin in us!* Because there is no moving forward, no getting free, until we admit that. Also, I may be stupid and stubborn in some areas of my life, but I am smart enough to know that I do not want to be the person who calls God a liar. I want his words to have a place in my heart. I don't want to be a fool; I want to be cleansed and forgiven. It seems that walking in the light with Jesus hinges on my ability to admit my sinfulness. He can't make me righteous until I admit that I am wrong.

Living in a culture that thrives on being in the right, we find it difficult to admit that we have been wrong. Living in a world in which each person claims to have his or her own personal truth and set of guidelines, we find it difficult to draw a bead on sin. Living in a society that thrives on darkness and celebrates depravity, we find it difficult to know how to step into the light. But if in the depths of our tired supergirl hearts, we want to walk in God's presence and taste the freedom he has to offer us, we have to quit hiding.

Zacchaeus realizes this while perching in a tree. His sin is hidden from no one but himself. In fact, as a tax collector, he is despised by most. He has swindled his countrymen in the past, has taken their cash, and is living off of the hard-earned, much-needed money of others. Zacchaeus is a mess. He is rich, but he is a mess. He isn't happy and he isn't free. Because if he was, he wouldn't keep needing to take more money or look for something or someone who meant more. He wouldn't be shimmying up a tree, surrounded by foliage (here we go with the foliage again), searching for answers.

Even though Zacchaeus is on the lookout for Jesus, he is still hiding. He wants to catch a glimpse of the Messiah, to see what all the fuss is about, without giving up his day job. I know he is a small man, but if he really wanted to see Jesus close up, he could have pushed his way to the front of the crowd. Zacchaeus isn't just short; he feels small inside. As far as sinning goes, he is a repeat offender, and everybody knows it. The weight of all he has done to his fellow men, the stealing, the lying, the conning, using his authority for evil, keeps him in hiding. So here he is, high from his leafy vantage point, trying to catch a glimpse of God, while not yet fully coming into the light. But Jesus doesn't play like that.

The crowd swells and pushes forward, massing around Jesus, moving him forward under the canopy of trees. Jesus stops and looks up and sees Zacchaeus peering at him between the branches.

> When Jesus came by, he looked up at Zacchaeus and called him by name. "Zacchaeus!" he said. "Quick, come down! For I must be a guest in your home today."
>
> Zacchaeus quickly climbed down and took Jesus to his house in great excitement and joy. But the crowds were displeased. "He has gone to be the guest of a notorious sinner," they grumbled.
>
> Luke 19:5–7

(The funny part of this Scripture is the crowd saying he is going to the house of a sinner when in fact any house he chose to go to would be a sinner's house. The other people just manage to keep their sin on the down low.)

Meanwhile, Zacchaeus stood there and said to the Lord, "I will give half my wealth to the poor, Lord, and if I have overcharged people on their taxes, I will give them back four times as much!"

Jesus responded, "Salvation has come to this home today, for this man has shown himself to be a son of Abraham. And I, the Son of Man, have come to seek and save those like him who are lost."

Luke 19:8–10

This is the truly beautiful part of the story. Jesus comes to seek and save the lost. He is looking for sinners. Just like God comes looking for Adam and Eve in the garden. He is looking for people stuck knee deep in wrongdoing. He is looking for tired supergirls who miss the mark on a spectacularly regular basis. He knows there is this darkness, this chasm of sin that separates us from our Creator, from our destiny. And he is the only one who can set it straight. He is on the lookout for people he can bring into the light.

Zacchaeus is excited. In all his wrongness, Jesus seeks him out and wants to hang out with him. That sets Zacchaeus free. Jesus doesn't have to point out his sin. Zacchaeus offers instead, "Look, I've done bad stuff, and I am going to set it right."

All along he has been sinning, he knows that. Why the sudden change of tune? Because of that crazy, mind-boggling love God has for him. He can't withstand all that good solid love. It does him in.

Romans 5:8 says, "But God showed his great love for us by sending Christ to die for us while we were still sinners."

When you are a mess and you know you are a mess and everyone else knows you are a mess and then God comes along and says, "I love you even when you are a mess," you are undone.

You can't stand to be separated any longer. We tired supergirls are no different. We try to hide who we really are, but God is calling us down from trees and out from behind juniper bushes. He is tracking us down in the midst of our sin and saying, "I want to go to your house. I want to hang out with you. I love you."

And we cave. Who can resist that kind of loving? God's brilliant-shining-I-love-you-in-spite-of-your-junk-kind-of-love.

A note to the repeat offender: it doesn't matter if it is the twenty-seventh time you have had to bring this particular thing into the light. Bring it on out again. It loses its power when it's in the light. It doesn't matter if your sin is small and petty or so big you feel it will crush you, get it out in the light. If you are not sure how, try Zacchaeus's method. Name it and claim it. Tell Jesus you did wrong stuff and you aren't going to anymore. And then grab a few of your favorite supergirls, who love you like crazy, and tell them the same. They will understand because the funny thing is that they have a lot of sin too. And as for the In-sin-erator, you can tell him to keep his game of hide-and-seek to himself because you've been found. By Jesus. And it just doesn't get any better than that.

**8**

# I AM JEALOUS
# OF MY FRIENDS

I have friends who are kind and talented. Supergirls who own their own businesses and have multiple degrees. They have lovely homes and beautiful families. I have friends who travel the world and see fantastic places and eat spectacular food. I have friends who have given their lives to the pursuit of Jesus, sacrificing comfort and pleasure for taking news of him to the deep reaches of the earth. My friend Leslie is a lawyer. Ever since she was a little girl she wanted to be a lawyer. She has a gift for seeing the truth in things and is willing to fight for it. Nothing has swayed her from her dream. I think she is, quite possibly, brilliant. I am not jealous of Leslie. I love her and I am truly amazed by her, but I am not jealous of her. I am not jealous of her because I do not want to be a lawyer. I would be a terrible lawyer. I can never tell who is telling the truth. I am way too naïve and gullible to be a lawyer.

So maybe I am not jealous of my friends after all and this chapter is all just a lot of hype because I wanted to tell you one more thing that was wrong with me. That would be great, wouldn't it? I would like that to be my reality. I would like to genuinely appreciate each and every person God has put in my life, the places he is leading them, and the gifts he has given them. I would like to think of myself as a gracious, tired supergirl who wishes good things on all people and hopes for joy and happiness to rain down on everyone around me. I try not to get caught up in comparing and contrasting my life with those who live around me. I know there is nothing to be gained by stacking up my life, my talents, my belongings, my family, or my dreams against those of the next person. But there is the odd occasion when it doesn't matter how much I know that, I still feel that hot stab of jealousy. Just this morning I had an envy-ridden moment. A pea-green fit of jealousy overtook me and zapped the joy out of my morning. For goodness' sake.

Ever since I was little, I have wanted to be a writer. I wrote stories and poems and more stories and more poems, because I have a love affair with words. It wasn't until I was in my twenties that I began pursuing my dream of being a published author. I was naïve enough to think, *Hey, I will show my stuff to someone and they will think, "Here it is! The answer to all we have ever been looking for in a writer! Brilliant!"*

I went to writers' conferences and talked with publishers. I met with agents. I submitted pieces for publication. And I was rejected. Over and over. One by one, they handed my dream back to me. And I got some really mean rejection letters. Really mean. But I knew this was my path. And while I would cry, with the mean letter in hand, inevitably I would sit back down at the computer and begin typing away again, because it was in me. I had this thing in my gut, moving me forward, writing. Every year my writer friends would say, "This is your year to get published."

And it wasn't. I had no jealousy issues with my friends who had gotten published before me, who were getting published continually, while I was not getting published at all.

It was the people who had joined the writing path after me and had gotten published before me that really made me go nuts. Take today, for instance. I heard of someone who apparently started writing a blog. Just a little here's-what-happens-in-my-day kind of blog. But apparently, three gazillion people read the blog and forwarded it to their four gazillion friends, and now because of this blog, which I'm sure is fantastic, this person is getting published. Because of a blog. Not years of heart-wrenching blood and guts writing, attending conferences, or sending out dozens of manuscripts, but a blog. Did I mention it was just a blog? Do you see, tired supergirls, the bitterness, the violent resentment, the inability to rejoice with another person who is passionate about the same thing that I am passionate about, that is pouring from me? That is jealousy. Now I said I am not jealous of my friends, but when I called my sister Erica to tell her about this travesty, she said, "Apparently, you are jealous of your friends, your enemies, and people you don't even know at all."

So we had a good laugh. And then I had to ask Jesus to forgive me because she is right. Why does she have to be right? I don't care about my friends who have lots of money or sparkling careers in neurobiology or those who spend time in the Amazon or work in journalism. I am so happy for them. I rejoice for them in their adventures and their successes. But there is this seven-year-old who lives in my head, Little Miss No Fair, who has this piercing whine, and for the love of all that is good and right, she cannot be silenced.

"Why does that person get published after writing a blog? No fair!"

Or, "Why don't I ever get the easy life, the good job, the attentive boyfriend, the [you put in the thing you are jealous of], the Barbie playhouse . . . blah, blah, blah . . . no fair!"

She's a killer, tired supergirls. Yes, she is. A joy killer. A hope killer. A gratitude killer. That whole "no fair" thing kills many a blessing that comes our way.

Jealousy is another word that needs to be defined for us supergirls. The type of jealousy I am talking about is not the type that rears up when we think our boyfriend is cheating on us or the type that God has for his relationship with us. The type of jealousy that has wormed its way into our superhearts is the type that is envious of the advantages that others have or that resents their successes. The type of jealousy that erupts when we think someone may displace us or our position in life. The kind of jealousy that hopes someone won't be more successful than we are or surpass us with their greatness. It's the type of jealousy that springs from a fear that they will be or are already better than us in some way or that they will accomplish more than we will.

This type of jealousy seems to lie low and bury itself until someone does something or has something that we have been longing for or pining for in our heart of hearts. It creeps in when someone succeeds and we begin to fear that they will overshadow us, or worse, make who we are seem obsolete. This jealousy mushrooms when someone leapfrogs over us and becomes the person we have dreamed of becoming. It can move us to think things or say things or even do things to try and stifle their success. It's pretty ugly. And in all of our maturity, we feel like shrieking, "Hey, no fair!" And then all there is left in our mouths is that ugly aftertaste of thinking, *I wish that was me.*

Jealousy will make us tired supergirls crazy. Crazy. Because when we are jealous, we decide to give up our life in the pursuit of someone else's. Now that sounds foolish, doesn't it, when you think about it. Here God has gone and created you as a unique and precious individual, a complete original with personality, gifts, and talents that are only yours. He has gone so far as to knit you together in your mother's belly and knows how many hairs he has on your head, even the gray ones, or falsely colored ones, as it may be. He thinks of you more often than there are grains of sand on the beach.

That is a whole lot of thoughts. But when we are jealous, we are saying that is not enough. Nope, we don't like this life that God has given us, this person we are; we would like someone else's life. Someone else's successes. Someone else's advantages. Someone else's path. And that jealousy can chase away any joy or hope that God has given us on our own path or journey. Jealousy is we supergirls saying, "I would like to choose crazy over contentment."

Because jealousy does make you crazy. You are filled with bitterness and envy over someone or something that would never have come your way in the first place. Herod is the perfect example of this. Herod, who I'm pretty sure never sought God or followed his precepts a day in his life, hears there is a baby being born who will be king. The Messiah. The savior of the Jewish people. And he loses it. Really loses it.

> Jesus was born in the town of Bethlehem in Judea, during the reign of King Herod. About that time some wise men from eastern lands arrived in Jerusalem, asking, "Where is the newborn king of the Jews? We have seen his star as it arose, and we have come to worship him."
>
> Herod was deeply disturbed by their question, as was all of Jerusalem. He called a meeting of the leading priests and teachers of religious law. "Where did the prophets say the Messiah would be born?" he asked them.
>
> "In Bethlehem," they said, "for this is what the prophet wrote:
>
> 'O Bethlehem of Judah, you are not just a lowly village in Judah, for a ruler will come from you who will be the shepherd for my people Israel.'"
>
> Matthew 2:1–6

Immediately, Herod is jealous. He loves the power he has being king. He doesn't want anyone messing with his kingly designs. He does not want there to be another king. He likes his cushy day job. He doesn't want to be supplanted by Jesus or anyone else. I'm sure Little Miss No Fair was lurking behind some palace corner, whining, "No fair! Why does he get to be king? Look at all these long, hard hours you have put into ruling this kingdom. Some little baby should not be able to ruin your life and all of your palace parties. You better get rid of him. So unfair!"

Immediately he begins to plot how he can get rid of Jesus. He tries to rope the wise men into helping him find out where Jesus is. When they won't, he winds up killing thousands of innocent babies in an attempt to stop Jesus from becoming king. It didn't matter that Jesus's kingdom is an entirely different kingdom than Herod is ruling. All he heard was that someone else was going to be king and he went crazy with jealousy. Only a crazy person would kill babies.

But we tired supergirls would never be that crazy, right? We would never kill somebody just because we were jealous. But we let our jealousy kill other things, like friendships and trust. We might sabotage their reputations with our words. We harbor jealousy in our hearts, and it kills grace and gratitude and love and our peace of mind. When we focus on the lives of others, instead of the life that God has given us, we lose perspective. And we lose more than that; we lose the ability to be grateful for all that God has already done in our lives. Unbeknownst to us, there is a secret weapon against the evil foe, Little Miss No Fair. Two little words send her into a downward spiral of doom. Thank you. That's it. Just thank you.

When we say thank you, we are refocusing on the person to whom we are giving thanks: Jesus. We don't have time to examine the lives of others, or dream about the greener grass on the other side of the fence, when we are concentrating on

Jesus. When we say thank you we are taking stock of what we have already been given, the blessings that have been poured out on us, the lives that we have been blessed with. We are recognizing all that God has done for us already and resting in the fact that he, above all, knows what life is best for us. Thank you for grace. Thank you for forgiveness. Thank you for the ability to breathe. Thank you for hope. Thank you for fuzzy socks and hot chocolate. Thank you for friends. The thank-yous go on and on. And with each thank-you, the "no fairs" seem to get a little quieter. The seven-year-old whiny girl retreats in defeat. The thankful tired supergirl triumphs. Because of Jesus. Funny thing, but that seems to be the way it always works.

9

I JUDGE PEOPLE

I love grace. I love that Jesus looks beyond my crud and loves me for me. I don't deserve grace, but I get it anyway. I love that he doesn't judge me based on my past sins. I love that I get to be free and there is no condemnation in Christ. His grace is fantastic. Amazing grace. I thank God for it. I sing songs about it. I want all the grace God has for me. Pour it on me! Truckloads of it. Right now. Grace is fantastic. But here's the thing . . . I love it so much that I may not have any left over for you. Sorry.

The funny thing is that even though God poured his grace out on me and doesn't judge me, somehow it's hard for me to pass the grace along. I am, in fact, a terrific judger. It's almost a gifting. Let's call it an unspiritual gift. I have a lot of unspiritual gifts, but I am particularly spectacular in the judging department. Try me. Just at a glance I can size up a room.

Take the Starbucks I am sitting in. Woman on the left with white blonde hair and tattooed shoulders? Ex-rocker chick, probably divorced, could have a chance as Kid Rock's new lady. Man on the right with greasy hair and tube socks pulled up to his knees? Newly paroled sex offender—note to self: keep keys at the ready in case I need to stab at his eyes if he accosts me in the parking lot. Teeny bopper barista? Cute girl, maybe smart, why is she not in school? Does her mother know she is working at Starbucks in the middle of the day? Maybe she has half days at school; either way, her mocha is spot on . . . God bless her. Do you see what I mean?

It's a gift. It comes naturally. I don't even try to judge people. It just flows from me.

And that is just judging by appearances. Don't even get me started on the people I actually know and interact with. Like my husband. After one of our very rare (weekly) discussions (fights) over how he has hurt me (I never hurt him) and how he needs to change (I am perfect the way I am), he said these words to me: "Susanna, I feel like you just don't have any grace for me."

Of all the terrible, truthful things to say to the woman who bore your unbelievably large children (all nine pounds and over). How could he say I have no grace? Maybe because he has lived with me for over ten years. That is a lot of years of towing the line. And I recognized in that instant what he has known all along. I don't have a whole lot of grace to pass around. Even for the ones I love best.

Why is it so hard for us supergirls to be grace givers? We want God's grace for ourselves, but we don't want to share it. We want the forgiveness, the pardon, the joy of living free. We want Jesus to pay the price for our sins, but we want others to pay the price for their own. We want to hang on to past hurts and point out other people's junk even though we want them to forgive the hurts we've caused them and excuse the junk that clutters our own lives.

Supergirls everywhere—beware of the Judge! He sits at the ready. Right within earshot, pounding his gavel and handing out judgments at will. Saying things like,

"Docket #43, last week Sally snubbed you at playgroup. She's no good. Don't forgive her. Four weeks snubbing minimum sentence."

"Case #71 being heard. Two years ago your boyfriend lied to you. Don't ever trust him again. He'll never change.

Sentence? Bring up his shortcomings every chance you get."

The Judge is ruthless. He never takes into account things like that maybe Sally was hurting and she didn't mean to be rude but she is quite possibly at the end of her rope. Or that your boyfriend was scared to tell you the truth and was afraid of how you would respond. There is no give in the Judge. He is absolutely graceless.

And here's the thing. It's not pretty. The judging. It is ugly and hard and Jesus is not in it. When Jesus talks to the crowd about judging during the Sermon on the Mount, he says,

> Don't do it. It's not good, and how you treat others will come back to haunt you.
>
> supergirl paraphrase

> Stop judging others, and you will not be judged. For others will treat you as you treat them. Whatever measure you use in judging others, it will be used to measure how you are judged. And why worry about a speck in your friend's eye when you have a log in your own? How can you think of saying, "Friend, let me help you get rid of that speck in your eye," when you can't see past the log in your own eye? Hypocrite! First get rid of the log from your own eye; then perhaps you will see well enough to deal with the speck in your friend's eye.
>
> Matthew 7:1–5

Personally, I prefer the verses before these ones that say I don't have to worry about what I wear or eat, that God will take care of me. I usually coast right by the judging verses, and read on to where Jesus says that if I ask, I will receive and that God gives good gifts to those who ask. But Jesus doesn't fool around when it comes to judging others. Because he knows, first, that he is the only one qualified to do it, and second, we aren't able to help others with their mess until we've dealt with our own.

I wear contacts. I love them. They are less cumbersome than glasses and I have far better peripheral vision when I wear them. I tried to get lasik surgery, but they told me my corneas were too thin. Too thin. A phrase that would have been a compliment in reference to my upper thighs, the backs of my arms, or my post-baby midriff, but I digress. I have skinny corneas, so I wear contacts.

The only downside to wearing contacts is when I get something caught under one of them. Heaven forbid that I get a piece of fuzz or a wayward eyelash trapped under one of them while I am driving, because I will go careening off of the road, clawing at my eye. It is excruciating. Everything stops. I can't move, I can't focus. I can't do a thing until I have ripped the contact out of my eye and gotten rid of the offending party. Supergirl or not, a strategically placed piece of sand has been known to incapacitate me for a good fifteen minutes. I'm not kidding. Don't get me started on the evils of fuzzy sweaters and airborne pollen. These microscopic terrors are a bane to contact wearers everywhere.

And according to Jesus, I am not dealing with a wee bit of fluff here. Apparently, I have a redwood sticking out of my eye. Not in the least bit microscopic. I have to agree it would be difficult to help someone else out with their piece of lint because I would be bumping into them with my tree. Jesus keeps bringing it back home. We have to take care of our own problems before pointing out other people's problems. We supergirls are incapacitated by a lovely forest of elms, poplars, and, my favorite, maples, which are sprouting from our retinas. We cannot see our way clear until we ask Jesus to help us with a little trimming.

And let's be honest. Would any of us actually have time to point out the sins of others if we were knee deep in resolving our own issues? The Judge is hemming and hawing, pounding away, trying to get our attention . . .

"Your co-worker is gossiping about you again! The sentence is . . ."

And you are saying, "Well, if it please the court, actually, I tend to gossip frequently myself and I was just asking God to help me in that area. . . ."

Or the Judge points a knobby finger at your boyfriend: "He lied to you again. Don't give him the chance to explain. Three years . . ."

And you cut him off, saying, "Well, actually, Judge, could you go easy on him because in high school, I skipped class once and wrote myself a note, pretending I was my mom, and my counselor called me in and . . ."

The Judge cuts in with a "Give me a break! Court will be in recess for however long it takes you to come to your senses and give these people what they deserve." You get the picture.

Then an unbelievable thing happens. When we focus on our own sins, our own struggles, our own inconsistencies, our own weaknesses, we tend to be softer toward others. And if by chance, we supergirls ask Jesus to begin clearing out the trees in our eyes, he will pour in grace and forgiveness, and the way we see others will begin to change. I think perhaps we will see each other the way he sees us. Through a lens of mercy and freedom and love. And as for the Judge? Case dismissed.

**10**
# I HAVE
# ANGER ISSUES

Some days I am a happy tired supergirl. Some days I am a melancholy tired supergirl. But today, today I am an angry tired supergirl. Angry. Mad. Irritated. Upset. Whatever word you want to use to frame the thought, that is me. Maybe it's the heat of this summer afternoon in my non–air-conditioned house. Maybe it's the fact that no matter how hard I try to block out time for writing, something interrupts me. Or maybe it's the twenty minutes I spent online, when I planned to be writing, trying to access a cartoon for my kids to watch and a website kept bouncing me back to the home page. Repeatedly. Or maybe it's the list that looms large in my head of all I want to squeeze into each day that is squeezing the life out of me right now. I'm sure it is all of these things and more.

I'm right there at boiling over. All the feelings of this sweltering day have been simmering inside of me. I've been trying to keep my anger buckled down. I've been trying to hold it in. That heady explosive thing in me. That feeling that I may not be able to control what comes out of my mouth. That something hot and wrong is brewing within my body and I am about to let loose on someone and tell them what I think about it. My anger tends to take the form of searing words.

Some supergirls let loose with their anger using their fists, raining blows on the world. Some supergirls turn it inward, letting it ruminate and harden and color their whole outlook with bitterness. Some supergirls are on the edge most days, barely hanging on by their finely manicured nails, and letting go with short blasts of scathing repartee to any hapless passerby. Some supergirls are so overheated with anger, they get cold and freeze everyone out with their chilly silence. And some of us supergirls let it build and build over days and weeks to a blowup of volcanic proportions, leaving chaos in our wake.

I have a vivid first memory of my anger. I was four years old.

I was trying to put on a plaid turtleneck, putting both my head and arm through the same opening, and I got stuck. And furious. My little body was tight with rage, and I screamed and cried and stayed in the vise-like grip of that turtleneck. I couldn't see my way clear, and I was beyond the normal itch of frustration. I remember I felt like I was about to burst from the inside out.

And that is how the grip of anger feels. It feels out of control and explosive, like a shaken-up bottle of Coke. The pressure builds and builds and then BAM! Here we go. And when it is all over, when the top has blown and the sticky spray is covering all that is around us, we supergirls are spent. And sad and ashamed. And left to clean up the mess we have made. Whether it is apologizing to our kids for letting sarcastic words fly at them like little stinging pellets or to our roommate for screeching about the dishes that can never find their way out of the sink. Our anger gives them an unforgettable show of the dark places in our not-so-super souls. There is always a mess to be cleaned up.

Because that is the way the Instigator likes it. Messy. He is that voice within your head. The voice that says yes to your anger. Yes to exploding. Yes to venting. Yes to screaming. Yes to throwing things. Yes to not thinking about what comes after the anger is over. Yes to fighting. Yes to the silent treatment. Yes to the mean looks and eye rolling. Yes to everything raw and unedited and cutting that you want to say. He wipes out the "inappropriate" sensor and gives the thumbs-up to your irrational, hurtful, untamed behaviors. He encourages you to feel the heat of being upset and go with it. He's not a whisperer. He has to have a loud voice to be heard above the roar of anger in your head. He likes to use key phrases like:

"How could he do that to you? Don't let him get away with that!"

Or "You are totally right to feel angry. Nothing ever goes your way."

He prods us to feeling justified in our wrath. And most definitely squelches the voice of reason or goodness or Jesus when you are in the angry situation.

There are different triggers that lead to anger. Mostly it is sparked by a negative event or emotion. Envy. Jealousy. Stress. Humiliation. Fear. Being wronged. An unkind word headed your way. Pain—both emotional and physical. Just the other day, I was head butted, by accident, mind you, by little boy number two. I was blinded by the unexpected pain. And I succinctly remember the voice of the Instigator saying, "Grab his head and squeeze it off."

And in my pain, it truly seemed the right thing to do. And as I reached for his curly blonde head, I had to mindfully think, *No, your second child needs his head. Leave it where it is.*

And I had to take long sucking breaths of air as I clutched my bruised cheekbone. It was reactionary.

Few of us supergirls are truly thinking when we are reacting. We are in the moment, acting out of our pain. The pain that comes from feeling out of control. Things are happening that we can't control, and we lash out because we don't like it. We don't want it. And we can't see our way clear to any good solution. Do you think that if we supergirls were thinking clearly, we would use words that hurt the tender hearts of our children, bruise close-knit relationships, and create gaps and rifts in our communication with the people who deeply care for us?

In Psalm 37:8, David says this: "Stop your anger! Turn from your rage! Do not envy others—it only leads to harm." And he was right. Anger left alone to find its own solution goes the way of violence. War, riots, divorce, murder are all born of anger. The Instigator wants us to look at a wrong situation and make it wrong-er.

But here's the thing. Anger in and of itself isn't wrong. It is an emotion. Like happiness or fear. We all have it in us. The craziness comes when our anger takes a left turn. The problem comes in the path we choose to follow when our anger blazes within us like a torch. So how is it that Jesus was righteous in his anger? How did he use that boiling feeling within him to bring about God's glory and rightness to something gone wrong? Jesus looked at a wrong situation and allowed his anger to help him make it right.

> Jesus entered the Temple and began to drive out the merchants and their customers. He knocked over the tables of the money changers and the stalls of those selling doves. He said, "The Scriptures declare, 'My Temple will be called a place of prayer,' but you have turned it into a den of thieves!"
>
> The blind and lame came to him, and he healed them there in the Temple.
>
> Matthew 21:12–14

Taking care of his Father's house is his business. He walks into the temple, this place that houses the presence of God himself. The religious folks are making a mockery and a mall out of this sacred place. This doesn't sit well with the Christ. In fact, he can't let it stay the way it is. He is seeing clearly in his anger. He is not blinded by his fury. He is propelled by it. And he begins sacking the courtyard. Throwing tables. Spilling money. Freeing doves. The merchants scatter, and the birds soar heavenward. And as the dust settles, as the passion of the moment is spent, something very right happens. Jesus begins healing people. He has righted the wrong. The temple is ready to do what it is meant to do: restore the people to right relationship with God. Jesus, God in skin, has walked into his house and set it to rights. That's good stuff.

And truly, we supergirls want to set things right as well. It is in the poor treatment of ourselves or of others that we supergirls are moved to anger. Nothing gets us steamed like when we see someone shamed or made fun of. Or when we are told we are less than we are. Or when we see a picture of a starving baby, pitiful and crying. We get furious. Violence against women? We are maddened. Children being molested? A seething, righteous anger pierces our hearts. And in these moments the voice of our Redeemer is loud.

The Instigator is saying, "Let's tear this place up."

Jesus is saying, "Let's make it what it was meant to be."

While the Instigator wants us to spend our anger on the pettiness of life, Jesus is inviting us to join him in using our anger to make life better. And while the Instigator would love the daily wrongs that rub against us to ignite into a raging fire, Jesus is wondering if we could let go of the anger that damages those around us and invites us to be angry with him about the things that matter. He would like us to get good and mad about babies that are too skinny, kids that have never met their dads, and people dying without knowing who he is. He is hoping we will rage against poverty, injustice, and people being mean to each other. And he would really like us to be a part of the solution.

Paul says it this way in Romans 12:21: "Don't let evil get the best of you, but conquer evil by doing good."

Jesus would love for us to do some good. To love some hurting people. And help some babies get fed. He would especially like us to give someone a glass of water or a piece of chocolate in his name. And then he would really appreciate it if we could conquer some evil. He promises to help us. And I think we can do it. After all, we are supergirls.

**11
I AM UNDISCIPLINED**

I would like to be able to tell you that I am disciplined. I would like to say that I have self-control. I would like to say that I am never late, I meet all expectations, I finish projects in a timely manner, and if I set my mind to something, I get it done. I would like to say all those things. But I would be lying. Instead I must say that I am usually late. This I blame on my children. I rarely meet my own expectations, and I am probably lacking in the area of others' expectations of me as well. I tend to procrastinate. On a regular basis. I struggle to keep committed to things like proper sugar intake and craft kits. I have a needlepoint pillow I began soon after I married. I now have three children. It is still incomplete. I have such good intentions. I really do want to live my life in a way that is excellent. And yet when it comes to following through, I am found lacking.

Take my exercise program. I know I need to exercise at least three times a week, more if possible. I know I need to be completing some kind of weight-bearing routine to keep myself from becoming a poster child for osteoporosis. I know that exercise gives you more energy and can help with depression. So really, exercising not only benefits you but the people you interact with. I know these things. And yet my knowing these things does not necessarily translate into my doing these things. My current exercise program is that I buy exercise videos. I don't actually do or even watch the videos. I just buy them. I have a nice row of shiny new DVDs lining my bookshelf. I see the infomercials on TV and I think, *Oh, that looks fun! I could do that. And they lost twenty-three pounds in only four days. The other five exercise videos I bought from the last five infomercials actually required me to exercise. But this one looks like I don't really have to exercise. I just have to dance around in cute workout gear and then I will look like that peppy cheerleader-type girl who is leading the class.*

Scott drew the line when the Perfect Gym arrived at the door. He could put up with me buying a few videos here and there, but when I purchased a piece of workout equipment that required three easy payments of $69.95 and claimed to give me abs of steel and thighs like a Greek goddess, all while folding down to a manageable size that could fit under my bed, he looked at me and said, "You know you're sending that back, right?"

"Yes."

"Good. I'm glad we're clear on that."

Because he knows that I am not serious about exercising. I would have been paying three easy payments of $69.95 to store something under my bed. I really want to be serious. I know it is good for my health and if I don't start lifting weights soon, I will lose all bone density and could possibly have one of those humps on my back when I am eighty. Why is it so hard to commit to something that is so beneficial? So life changing?

I'll let you in on a little tired supergirl secret. Exercising is hard. And you sweat a lot. It requires stomach muscles and focus. Those are two things I am generally low on. After birthing three children, I don't have any stomach muscles left. I am core-less. My biceps are okay since I tote small children and giant baskets of laundry around all day, but if you asked me to run a mile, I would collapse with hideous side cramps after a block or two. And yet I still long to be fit. I want to be strong and have energy and ward off depression. But really, what I would like more is to have all the benefits of exercise without having to get up off of my couch. If I could figure out a way to do this, I would. Really, I would.

We tired supergirls would like to receive the benefits of living a disciplined life without actually having to discipline ourselves. While we may do fine at disciplining our children, setting boundaries and objectives, it is much more difficult to say no to ourselves. We would love to say no to ourselves— really, we would. Starting tomorrow. But as for today, this supergirl really needs that fat rich piece of chocolate heaven sitting in a pool of raspberry puree, topped with a dollop of real whipped cream. Who cares that your arteries are clogging just breathing in the aroma of all that chocolate goodness? The foil of the disciplined life is the Procrastinator. He agrees with you that discipline is important and that it really would add to your life. He just thinks you don't need to worry about it right now. Maybe next Thursday, but today you should go right ahead and indulge yourself. He says things like, "Oh for goodness' sake, don't worry about the money. It will all work out in the end. Bankruptcy is not that big of a deal."

Or, "Bible reading is overrated. Just get one of those mugs with a Scripture verse on the side and drink your coffee out of it. That works just as well. Start your Bible reading plan next Tuesday. Don't beat yourself up about it."

Or in my case, "It is quite possible to be in fantastic physical shape while remaining totally inert on your sofa. You are completely prepared to compete in a triathlon if you *wanted* to. You just don't *want* to. That's all. You can start exercising in the summer. That will give you the next six months to build up to it."

The Procrastinator would love for us to remain exactly as we are. He would like to stunt the growth process, whether it is spiritual, physical, or emotional. He is against all kinds of things that require planning and foresight. He wants you stuck in the here and now.

Any runner is a planner. You may see people jogging around the park, footloose and fancy free, or so you think. But they are jogging with a goal in mind. Whether it is one mile or five, there is a course that they set out upon; they pace themselves and they go for it. Maybe they are training for a marathon or maybe they run every morning to keep their blood pressure down, but I guarantee you that the whole time they are running, they are not thinking, *Hey, this is fantastic. I had no idea this was going to happen. I am running. The wind is in my hair. The pavement is slapping beneath my feet. I feel great.*

There are moments when they do feel fantastic. There are moments when the endorphins kick in and there is no other place on God's green earth they would rather be. But then there are the moments when the blister begins to form on the back right heel and each step feels like fire. Or there are the stabbing side cramps that come from not getting enough oxygen on a cold winter's morning. Or there are the moments when they think, *Why am I not sitting by the fire, sipping a latte right now?*

The body begins to speak loudly, and it is up to the spirit to say, "I am doing this for a reason. I am pressing on for a reason. I am continuing this painful process for a reason." The goal outweighs the momentary suffering. And that only comes from being disciplined. From being able to see past the momentary to the eternal or at least to next year. This runner is running because she knows that what awaits her at the end of the run is far better than what awaits her if she sits on her couch and watches exercise infomercials.

Being disciplined is not so much denying ourselves the things that we like as it is about adding to our lives. Discipline enables us to do more. To be more. Because if you can run one mile this week, you will probably be able to run two next week. And if you put one hundred dollars into savings each month, you will more than likely have some savings at the end of the year. And if you are able to say, "No, I will not have that chocolate piece of heaven with raspberry puree and whipped cream loveliness, even though it has my name engraved on it in chocolate sprinkles," you may be able to keep yourself from the diabetic heritage that precedes you. When we supergirls are disciplined, we are not denying ourselves, we are investing in our future. And despite what advice the Procrastinator spews our way, it is a good thing to begin investing today. Not tomorrow or next Wednesday or four leap years from now, but today.

Paul looks at it like this:

> Remember that in a race everyone runs, but only one person gets the prize. You also must run in such a way that you will win. All athletes practice strict self-control. They do it to win a prize that will fade away, but we do it for an eternal prize. So I run straight to the goal with purpose in every step. I am not like a boxer who misses his punches. I discipline my body like an athlete, training it to do what it should. Otherwise, I fear that after preaching to others I myself might be disqualified.
>
> 1 Corinthians 9:24–27

Paul talks about disciplining himself so that he can share the gospel to the best of his ability. He knows that if he wants to achieve his goal of reaching the Jews, the Gentiles, the oppressed, the free, he has to set his sights on a goal. The prize. If not, he is going to miss out. He has to train himself to do what he should. Which brings to mind the thought that self-discipline is not something that comes naturally to Paul either. Which I find to be encouraging to us supergirls who become so easily distracted from the prize at hand.

It seems discipline is not something that just springs up within the breast and is easily obtained. Could anything be more difficult than saying no to something you truly long for, like hot chocolate chip cookies fresh from the oven, a sparkly shirt on sale, or just thinking of yourself instead of considering others? No, I don't think so. It goes against the grain to think long term instead of short term, which is the very essence of discipline. It is not easy to practice self-control. Discipline is unnatural. It is not in our nature. But when we ask Jesus to come in and change our lives and make us more like him, that can change.

Peter talks about it like this:

> As we know Jesus better, his divine power gives us everything we need for living a godly life. He has called us to receive his own glory and goodness! And by that same mighty power, he has given us all of his rich and wonderful promises. He has promised that you will escape the decadence all around you caused by evil desires and that you will share in his divine nature.
>
> So make every effort to apply the benefits of these promises to your life. Then your faith will produce a life of moral excellence. A life of moral excellence leads to knowing God better. Knowing God leads to self-control. Self-control leads to patient endurance, and patient endurance leads to godliness.
>
> 2 Peter 1:3–6

We tired supergirls do not simply decide one day that we will live a life of discipline or that we will exercise self-control in our lives. It begins with faith, pure and simple. When we believe in Jesus, we get to share in his divine nature, which is so very unlike our own nature. He alone gives us the power we need to live a disciplined life. As we begin to cling to his promises, we get to know God better. Knowing God leads to self-control.

This is exactly what the Procrastinator is afraid of. He is vastly afraid that we will get up off of our proverbial couch and tap into Jesus and his divine power. Because if we do, then for goodness' sake, we might be able to live the life we were designed for. We will be able to see the prize for what it is. We will be able to see past the momentary temptations to the eternal goal. We will be able to run with endurance and with strength. His strength. And we will be able to finish this race, this path that has been set before us with integrity and—do we even dare say it—victory. And that is far better than a chocolate piece of heaven. Even with a dollop of whipped cream on top.

# 12
# I GET TOO BUSY
# FOR GOD

I have already confessed that I am tired. I have perma-color dark circles under my eyes. And let it be known that I am so utterly exhausted because I live in America, and here in America, it is un-American to not be busy. In other countries, people like to lounge a bit. They have month-long vacations in the summer and drink tea in the afternoon. I want to move there because I am growing tired of being so tired. I start the day feeling like I am running late. Even if I woke up at four in the morning, I would feel like I had a late start. I get my kids up and prod my husband. Mass mayhem follows as we get three little boys dressed, fed, dressed again because a bottle of syrup has worked its way into sticky trails all over three sets of little boy shirts and pants. (Side note: someone needs to design a full-body bib. I once let the boys eat without their shirts on thinking this would solve the spillage problem, but they kept trying to lick food off their bare chests . . . but I digress.) And this is just the first hour of the morning.

Then the serious "busy" is underway. Every single day is filled to the brim with busy. And not just general busy. Not frivolous busy like reality TV and eating cupcakes. This is really good busy stuff. This kind of busy will make the world a better place. A happier place. At least that's what I tell myself.

There is kid busy. There is school. There is preschool. There are diapers and more diapers. There is cleaning. There is laundry. Way too much laundry. So much laundry my eyes well up with tears when I think of the laundry. There are playgroups, parent meetings, and school fund-raisers. There is helping in the classroom and subbing at the preschool. There are childhood pictures to be taken and parks to be visited. There is homework, and tired supergirls, beware. You thought when you got out of school, when you had that college diploma in hand, that your homework days were over. Not so. When your kids have homework, once again, you have homework. People need to tell other people these things so that people can prepare themselves for the devastation of having homework again. There are three meals and thirteen snacks to be made each day. And thirteen snacks is not that many. Sometimes kids want fifteen snacks a day. There are books to be read, games to be played, and friends to have over.

And there is work busy. I organize other people's lives because, goodness knows, mine is a mess. That entails scheduling and childcare and organization so that I can leave my unorganized house to go organize someone else's house. And there is writing. Somewhere in all my craziness, I must find a quiet moment and a clean table to put my computer on so that I can try to pull together some semblance of order out of my scattered brain and write with wittiness and hope.

Then there is church busy. There is house prep for gatherings at our house. There is setup at the theater on Sunday when everyone meets for our large gathering. There is worship practice. There is Sunday school prep. There is the actual service. There is the occasional mom's group and ladies' night out. There are retreats and denominational meetings. There are missions trips and community outreaches. We don't play around when it comes to church.

Now, really, tired supergirls, must I go on? I didn't even mention trying to set aside time for dating my husband, one-on-one time with the kids, getting together with friends, planting flowers, doing the bills, or sleeping. Did I mention sleeping yet? Oh, and Jesus. For goodness' sake, how could I forget to mention finding time for Jesus? I guess it would be because I am so very busy that I frequently forget that I must make time for the Savior of my soul. And somehow, some way, he seems to be the one person I don't ever write down in my organizer. When I'm actually using my organizer. Sometimes I forget to use it when I am so busy.

Supergirls everywhere are struggling to find a balance between work, family, church, friends, and Jesus. We are cramming our lives full to overflowing and we can barely breathe. There are so many good, valid, important things to be done along with the fact that we just don't know how to order our lives, how to maximize our potential, or how to accomplish all that needs to be accomplished.

That's when Miz Do Good enters the picture. She is the rules-and-regulations gal that lives in your head. She likes to help you out in your Christ-following journey, saying things like, "If you read five chapters of Scripture, then you're good. Three? Not so good. No Bible reading this week? You're on the fast track to the fiery pit of destruction."

Or she'll mention church attendance. "Wow, so you think you're doing okay with just Sunday mornings? That's interesting. You may want to rethink that."

And she also likes the saying "How can you say no?"

She can be very encouraging about your acts of Christ-likeness. Reminding you of all the goodness that you are already pouring yourself into, like that time you spent with your grandma at the nursing home or the run for cancer you did with your group from work. But then she just likes to ask little questions like, "But what about the orphans in

Ethiopia? You should probably go on that missions trip. How can you say no to something that important?"

Or she'll mention something like, "You've been doing a fantastic job reading to your kids, but what about your friend Rita? She needs you to be more available. You better figure out how to spend some more time with her."

But that is where the direction ends, because she likes to be vague. She doesn't seem to know how you will squeeze in three more things onto your be-more-like-Jesus to-do list. But she knows that you can absolutely handle three more things, maybe even four. She has great faith in your ability to save the world, single-handedly, and still have time for devotions.

My mom told me that when she was little, she was taught that the word *JOY* stands for *J*esus, *O*thers, and *Y*ou. She used to sing it in a song about how joy equals putting Jesus first, then sandwiched in the middle you put others, and then whatever you do, put yourself last and you will have joy. Like the three slices of the proverbial pie of how to live your life. But if that is the case, does housecleaning fit in under the "you" category because you like having your house clean or the "others" category because you are clearing a path from the living room to the bathroom so that "others" can get through? And which part of the pie should go for that budget you need to finish at work and that charitable book drive you agreed to help out with? And there is only so much pie, you know.

Besides that, the world at large is telling us supergirls that we need some *me* time. That we have neglected our own needs and we need good boundaries and such, so that our lives can be more productive. So maybe we shouldn't put ourselves last because if we don't care for ourselves, then how can we care for others? So how much of your life's pie is allocated to *me* time? Does *me* time include the times when a tired supergirl is sitting in her cubicle at work by herself? Because if not, we are going to have to pencil it in around 1:27 in the morning, when we are fast asleep, because the rest of our day is jam-packed with business meetings, family meal times, and a workout session with Helga, our personal trainer. And as for Jesus, we think he needs a whole pie dedicated just to him because our real-life pie has no slices left. Supergirl alert! You can't do it all. Nope! It just cannot be done.

Forget the whole pie thing. If we are endlessly slicing our pies, at the end of the day, all we supergirls have left to offer Jesus is a few crumbs. Time with God can't be something we try to squeeze in between, say, 2:00 and 2:27 in the afternoon. We can't just offer up a chunk of time to the God of the universe. We have to offer him ourselves. All of us. All of our time. We can't look at spending time with God as a set "devotional time." We have to emulate the one who came in the flesh and looked at spending time with God as a "devotional life."

Jesus modeled complete devotion to God. He was available to God all day long. Any time of day or night, he was ready. Just give the word and he was willing to go, do, be, say whatever God had for him at that moment. That included attending weddings or teaching in the synagogue. He wasn't boxed in by a certain amount of minutes spent in prayer or the weekly couple of hours spent in a pew or by what other people thought he should be doing for God.

The Pharisees, the Miz Do Goods of their time, tried to get Jesus locked into their God time frame. They wanted him to keep the Sabbath holy. That is what their religious culture had designated as "Time for God." It is all laid out neatly in the Ten Commandments: "Remember the Sabbath day and keep it holy."

In Luke 6:6–11, the story of Jesus's thoughts on the Sabbath unfolds:

On another Sabbath day, a man with a deformed right hand was in the synagogue while Jesus was teaching. The teachers of religious law and the Pharisees watched closely to see whether Jesus would heal the man on the Sabbath, because they were eager to find some legal charge to bring against him. But Jesus knew their thoughts. He said to the man with the deformed hand, "Come and stand here where everyone can see." So the man came forward. Then Jesus said to his critics, "I have a question for you. Is it legal to do good deeds on the Sabbath, or is it a day for doing harm? Is this a day to save life or to destroy it?" He looked around at them one by one and then said to the man, "Reach out your hand." The man reached out his hand, and it became normal again! At this the enemies of Jesus were wild with rage and began to discuss what to do with him.

Jesus kept messing with the religious folk. Asking them to think. Showing them that time with God isn't limited to one day and one day only. And time for God certainly doesn't revolve around keeping a set amount of rules or social mores. Time with God is about healing and giving life, not about keeping rules or maintaining others' expectations.

The masses had designs on Jesus too. They had big plans for him. They weren't out to destroy him like the Pharisees; they just wanted to suck the life out of him with all of their needs and their expectations.

In Luke 4:42–43, Jesus is on the move. He gets away from the thick of things to have some alone time. He has just finished a tour of casting out demons and healing every person he touched, and the passage says,

Early the next morning Jesus went out into the wilderness. The crowds searched everywhere for him, and when they finally found him, they begged him not to leave them. But he replied, "I must preach the Good News of the Kingdom of God in other places, too, because that is why I was sent." So he continued to travel around, preaching in synagogues throughout Judea.

It's interesting that he is very much aware of his purpose, of who he is and where he should be at any given moment. When the people think he should be worshiping, he is partying; when they think he should be out performing miracles, he is by himself praying. A lot of us supergirls think, *If I get my devotions in before I head off for work, I can check that off of my to-do list.*

Jesus didn't knock off a thirty-minute window and think, *Well, that's done. I've spent my time with God for the day.*

Nor did he crumble at the expectations of others, thinking, *I've really let these Samaritans down. I better cast out a few more demons to get them off my back.*

He spends time in the wilderness. He spends time at parties. He spends time healing people. He spends time sleeping. He spends time visiting with friends, and he spends time utterly alone. And all of it, he spends aware that he is in God's presence and that God is working in him, through him, and ultimately, he even gives his last breath so that we supergirls might do the same.

We tired supergirls like to have a system. We are looking to make our lives meaningful by the things we do, whereas Jesus's life was meaningful because of who he was. The things he did, the miracles he performed, the teachings he gave, the love that poured out from him, came from the fact that his whole being was immersed in the presence of God—all day, every day. And the whole process of being jailed, crucified, and resurrected from the dead means that we also can be immersed in the presence of God—all day, every day. Since Jesus took on our sinfulness and gave us his righteousness, there is nothing keeping us from hanging out with God, being available to him, and being who God meant us to be. We no longer have to try and cram him into one neat little section of our day; we can let him overflow into every nook and cranny of our year. We can open ourselves up to his direction, his presence, his peace from Monday morning in the office through Sunday evening small group. We don't have to rely on what other people think we should be doing or how much time we should allot to our spiritual upkeep.

If we are immersing ourselves in God's presence, letting him in on all of our business, we can tell Miz Do Good to take a hike. Then we supergirls can ask our heavenly Father what it is exactly that he would like us to be doing on this fine day, whether that is staying up all night praying for our co-worker whose marriage is on the rocks or going to an eighties party with big hair and Kool and the Gang blaring in the background. And then just like Jesus, instead of being overwhelmed by the busyness of life, we can go about doing our Father's business. And that would be super.

# 13
# I AM SELFISH

I am saying it loud and clear, people. I am selfish. While I would like to deny it, it is the truth. I am a self pleaser. Now, I'm not saying it proudly. That would be like saying with great jubilation, "I have corns."

That just doesn't make a whole lot of sense. Corns are no good. Just the fact that they are located on your feet and are called "corns" makes me feel a little nauseous. Things named after vegetables and one's feet should not be allowed to mingle. The same could be said about selfishness and the tired supergirl. Selfish is the very last thing on earth I wish to be. Or at least it is the very last thing on earth I want others to think about me. I want to be seen as generous, loving, and hospitable. I definitely don't want to be viewed as selfish. Self-ish. Consumed with one's self. Loving one's self over all others. Taking care of one's person before casting a thought toward anyone else. And yet, that is what I do most days. Think a whole lot about myself. In fact, this whole book is about myself. See how very selfish I am? So very full of myself. It's sickening, I know. Every day when I get up, I think about myself. What should I wear? What should I eat? What should I do? How can I get through my to-do list? Do you see it? Me? Myself? I? A whole lot of thinking being done about myself.

Now mind you, being a mother, I don't get to be as selfish as I want. I have to start thinking about the boys almost as soon as my eyes open. *What will they wear? What will they eat? How can I get Jack to stop wiping syrup on his pants before he goes to school?* As a parent, I am forced to be unselfish. But it's not because I awaken with thoughts of how I long to care to the best of my ability for those small humans God has entrusted to me. The whole unselfish thing goes against my nature. Selfishness comes so easily to me. I would much rather sit down for a cup of coffee than whip up little boys' breakfasts and comb down cowlicky hair and change diapers. I can't lie. I do like the good-morning kisses. But then again, we are back to thinking about my own likes and dislikes. So those kisses fit in quite nicely with my selfish self. Kisses for me. Coffee for me. Time for me. Oh, how I love me.

Selfishness is the Achilles' heel of tired supergirls every-where. We just can't stop thinking about ourselves. The world does tend to revolve around ourselves. We view everything through a me-colored lens. How will this affect me? Need I remind you, this is the very type of thinking that got Eve in heaps of trouble? Here she was in a garden of perfection, her every whim and need met, and she started thinking, *Why doesn't God want* me *to eat that apple? What harm could it do* me *for goodness' sake?*

Then the Snake came along and encouraged her to follow her inner diva. He encouraged her to ignore the instructions God gave her and treat herself to that gorgeous apple. Because what she wanted was more important than anything else, right? And so began the long, arduous journey of the first tired supergirl. Poor Eve. Or should I say, poor us? Because just like Eve, it is our daily struggle to cast aside the loud voice of the Diva. Her convincing words often over-shadow the words of the One who can show us who to be and fill us with who he is. The Diva's voice, for some reason, sounds exactly like my voice. Go figure. That is why I listen to her so often. She is so very smart and only wants what is best for, you got it, me. She is never lacking in opinions and makes a whole lot of sense almost all of the time. I really love the Diva a whole lot. That is why it is so very hard to fight against her. Because I feel like I am slugging it out with myself. Which, of course, I am.

So many tired supergirls get tripped up by the Diva because she is so persuasive. She even likes to put words in God's mouth and say things like, "God wouldn't want you to do anything that makes you uncomfortable. He really wouldn't. You need to think of yourself."

Or, "Once you take care of your own needs, you will be better equipped to take care of others. You really need to put yourself first."

The Diva coined the phrase "me time." I'm not really sure, but I think that phrase may be as nauseating to God as the word *corns* is to me. Because the phrase "me time" places you at the center of the universe and requires everything else to orbit around you. This is not what we are designed for. I have a sneaking hunch that celebrity, for all of its glory and perks, was the brainchild of the Diva. And we tired supergirls (those of us who read inappropriate gossip magazines while waiting to buy our groceries) know what celebrity is good for. Nothing. A whole lot of problems occur when the world revolves around the whims of a rock star or a child actor or a novelist hopped up on fame. And those crazy paparazzi—they can't be helping matters any. Reality is skewed for celebrities. They think the world lives and breathes for them. And they suffer for it, even if they don't realize it. They may not see it. But we tired supergirls do. We can easily recognize the destructiveness of the Diva in others. But somehow it is harder to recognize it in ourselves. The desire of the supergirl heart to follow after Jesus is at direct odds with the natural state of the heart, which is to listen to the Diva. We see this so clearly when Jesus talked to his disciples about his impending death.

> From then on Jesus began to tell his disciples plainly that he had to go to Jerusalem, and he told them what would happen to him there. He would suffer at the hands of the leaders and the leading priests and the teachers of religious law. He would be killed, and he would be raised on the third day.
> But Peter took him aside and corrected him. "Heaven forbid, Lord," he said. "This will never happen to you!"
> Jesus turned to Peter and said, "Get away from me, Satan! You are a dangerous trap to me. You are seeing things merely from a human point of view, and not from God's."
>
> Matthew 16:21–23

Now those are some harsh words for our good friend Peter. After all, he loves Jesus a whole lot. Peter recently revealed he believed that Jesus was the Messiah, the Son of the living God. So, it is a little bit comical that he takes Jesus aside to correct him. But for this moment, he thinks he may know a thing or two more than the one who fashioned the world and galaxies with a word. Which is basically what we supergirls do each time we decide to follow our own path. It's not that we don't love Jesus; we really do. We appreciate what he has done on our behalf, but obviously he is not quite up to speed on our situation, and we would like to help him out, take things in our own hands, and work things out in a way that will benefit ourselves. Peter does not want Jesus going anywhere.

He really likes having him around.

As for Jesus, he responds in the only way he can. He recognizes that voice caught up in the midst of Peter's words that tempts him, saying, "Think only of yourself." The voice that calls us to turn away from God's plan and seek our own plan.

The voice that seduced Eve in the garden. That is the voice of the Snake, Satan himself. And he recognizes that voice because, for goodness' sake, Satan tormented him for forty days in the desert, and as God's eternal Son, he was there the day that Satan was thrown out of heaven and witnessed him tripping up Eve in the garden. If he didn't give in to that voice in the desert, he isn't about to be trapped by it now. He is obeying God. He is centering himself around God. He is denying himself. Surely Jesus does not want to die on the cross, but he is going forward in the belief that the plan God has for him is the one and only plan that matters. He goes on to address the disciples.

> If any of you wants to be my follower, you must put aside your selfish ambition, shoulder your cross, and follow me. If you try to keep your life for yourself, you will lose it. But if you give up your life for me, you will find true life. And how do you benefit if you gain the whole world but lose your own soul in the process? Is anything worth more than your soul?
>
> Matthew 16:24–26

Losing your soul. This is the destructiveness of the Diva that we supergirls recognize so readily in others. The Diva would like to destroy any chance we have at real living. When we turn from God and follow after that voice—the one that is so alluring, the one that seems so logical and right, that snaky voice in the garden—we lose our souls. It is as simple as that. It is only when we put aside our selfish ambition and follow Jesus that we get our life back. We were created to be centered around God. For intimacy with him. For following after him. We don't really fancy taking up a cross. It sounds uncomfortable and difficult. That's not really our idea of a good time. And that is what the Diva is counting on.

She is hoping that we supergirls will want to keep our lives for ourselves. She is hoping we won't realize that the cost of following God's plan is worth it. She doesn't want us to recognize that the cross symbolizes freedom. It symbolizes the burying of our sin and the promise of new life. Taking up the cross and following after Jesus, no matter how difficult it may be at times, far outweighs any momentary satisfaction we may have putting ourselves first.

It is in that moment when we choose to give up our lives that the Diva just can't stand to be around anymore. The moment when we say no to our selfish nature and say yes to being a disciple, the Snake's voice begins to fade and the Diva goes into hiding. And we can begin to live. Jesus said that he came so that we might have life and have it abundantly. I think we should take him up on it.

14
I AM LONELY

I have three children. Three very small children. Three very small children who love me very much. If they could, they would Velcro themselves to my legs and go everywhere with me. I rarely have a moment to myself. I often sleep with one or two of them wedged under my arms or breathing into my neck. They love to find me by myself so they can get a little one-on-one time with me. They eat with me, dress with me, play with me, cry with me, and laugh with me. I often leave the door unlocked to the bathroom, in case somehow, in the brief time that it takes me to use the facilities, one of them were to maim themselves or lose a limb, they would be able to get access to me quickly. They have taken this as an open invitation to come sit down and have a chat. If it wasn't forbidden, they would bring snacks. I shouldn't be lonely with 24/7, around-the-clock sweet boys who can't seem to get enough of me. But I am.

I used to think the pit of loneliness that yawned within could only be filled with romance. I was forever looking for *the one*. And then I found *the one*. And no doubt about it, Scott is absolutely fantastic. He's funny. He's cute. He loves Jesus. And best of all, Scott's mine. For so many years, I searched for someone to be mine. Finally, here is someone who is not anyone else's. Someone who longs for time with me. Someone who gets me. Who laughs and cries with me. Someone who sees all the messes I have made in my life and still loves me. That is no small thing. I should not be lonely with a man like this. But I am.

I remember my mom telling me a story about her and my dad. They got married and three weeks later left family and friends in sunny California for grad school and the golden cornfields of Illinois. She said they cried all the way there. Even though they were head over heels in love and couldn't get enough of each other. She said she would have gone to the ends of the earth for him. And she did. The Midwest is very far from California. Then she told me that in one of her loneliest moments, she said to my dad, "I thought you would be enough for me . . . but you're not." I think it came as a surprise. When you are deeply in love with someone, you think, *This is it. The pit is gone. I'll never be lonely again.*

But then there it is again. Begging to be filled, for goodness' sake.

Some of us tired supergirls are lonely for good solid girlfriends. We crave the laughter, the sisterhood, the understanding. Some of us hanker after sweethearts. We long for intimacy and male affirmation. We want to take care of someone and to be taken care of. Some of us simply cannot wait to wrap our arms around a baby. We are lonely for a little one of our own. Some of us tired supergirls would kill for a somewhat normal family. A parent who checked in on us, was proud of us, and knew us inside and out. Some of us would love to find someone to mentor us. We are lonely for wisdom and empathy and comradeship. Some of us would just like to find *one* person. *Any* person in all the many persons in this world who would truly get us, inside and out. We are worn out by loneliness, and we will do whatever we need to do to fill that growing chasm within.

We are designed for relationships, pure and simple. There are many lonely shaped holes that dot our superhearts. We are always searching for that kindred spirit. The one who knows us. The one who loves us best.

Loner Chick is totally against us figuring out how to fill up the lonely pit. She gives helpful tips like: "So you know that you will always be lonely, right? No one is ever going to love you the way you need to be loved. Just give it up."

Or, "We've been down this road before. People are always a disappointment. You are never going to get what you need from him. He's great and all, but he's not *the one*."

Or, "You thought she was your best friend, but obviously she feels differently than you do. You're better off protecting yourself. She will only let you down."

Now the crazy thing about depressing Loner Chick is that part of what she says is true. We hear the rightness of what she says, and we tired supergirls believe it wholeheartedly. We really will be alone. We will be disappointed by people over and over again. They are just so human. So broken. Just like we are. So this half-truth makes us think that we will never be full. We will never truly feel that we are known and loved. We will never banish the loneliness. And the thing is, we tired supergirls can't. We haven't the ability to fill ourselves up. We are so used to being self-sufficient, to meeting our own needs, that we feel desperate that we don't have the power to fill that chasm on our own. What Loner Chick neglects to tell us is that there is One who can fill us. There is One who, in fact, longs to fill us up. He would like to fill in the chinks and nooks and crannies and pits of loneliness found in our hearts and souls. This is the whole reason that Jesus came to earth. To reestablish a right relationship with God the Father. Ever since Eve, this relationship had been broken, off-kilter, spoiled. Sin had destroyed that perfect, filling relationship between God and his creation.

As Jesus talks to his disciples about his purpose here on earth, about all that they have done together, he tells them soon they will not be together. This seems so strange to the disciples. They have been together for three years. They love this man. They would follow him to the ends of the earth. What can he possibly mean?

> But the time is coming—in fact, it is already here—when you will be scattered, each one going his own way, leaving me alone. Yet I am not alone because the Father is with me.
>
> John 16:32

And then as he finishes telling them these things, he says this amazing prayer over them. The Son of God is praying on their behalf. Because he wants these men to have the same kind of relationship with his Father that he has. The kind they were created for. The intimate garden relationship God intended for all of us way back in Eden before everything went so terribly wrong. Jesus wants them to know they are not alone. They don't ever have to be alone again.

> My prayer is not for the world, but for those you have given me, because they belong to you. And all of them, since they are mine, belong to you; and you have given them back to me, so they are my glory! Now I am departing the world; I am leaving them behind and coming to you. Holy Father, keep them and care for them—all those you have given me—so that they will be united just as we are. During my time here, I have kept them safe. I guarded them so that not one was lost, except the one headed for destruction, as the Scriptures foretold.
>
> And now I am coming to you. I have told them many things while I was with them so they would be filled with my joy. I have given them your word. And the world hates them because they do not belong to the world, just as I do not. I'm not asking you to take them out of the world, but to keep them safe from the evil one. They are not part of this world any more than I am. Make them pure and holy by teaching

them your words of truth. As you sent me into the world, I am sending them into the world. And I give myself entirely to you so they also might be entirely yours.

John 17:9–19

Now the thing that is missing in us, that intimacy, that love, that need to be full, can only be fulfilled by Christ. But these disciples do not know this. They don't know they cannot have full access to God the Father until Jesus takes on the punishment of their sins. They do not realize that Jesus is saying, "I love these people so much I want them to have what I have. Communion with you, Father. Fellowship with you. Full relationship with you." And Jesus is telling his Father that he is willing to do whatever it takes so that this can happen. He is giving himself entirely over to God's plan of salvation so that his disciples can be entirely God's. He is willing to die so they don't have to be lonely anymore. Even though Jesus is going back to heaven, he is making a way for his disciples to be full. To know love. To have a relationship with the Creator of their souls. He did that for them. He did that for us.

We tired supergirls will never find all we are looking for in the relationships we have here on earth. We aren't meant to. We weren't made to. We will only find what our souls hanker for in the presence of our heavenly Father. And what was once impossible is now possible because of Jesus. Because we belong to Jesus, we belong to the Father. *Belong* is just about the most opposite word to *lonely* that there is. Loner Chick has no clue what it feels like to belong. She skims the outskirts of real living and is empty and afraid to step into a real relationship. She is desperate to keep you from realizing there is a solution to the emptiness. She would really like to keep you on the sidelines of love.

The only way a tired supergirl can get rid of the lonely is to sink into the knowledge that she belongs to God. Wholly. Fully. Forever. Because Jesus loves us, because he died for us, we get to belong to God. Body and soul. The one who crafted us inside our mother's bellies, the one who designed our personalities and formed our souls, is waiting to fill us to running over with himself. And even better, he promises to never leave us or forsake us. And that is something that could, quite possibly, fill a tired supergirl's heart to overflowing.

# 15

# WISH LIFE WAS EASY

I dream about having easy days. I dream that I will wake up in the morning and everything will go exactly as I planned it in my head. I dream about days when the children obey, my husband and I communicate well, and someone is handing out free chocolate. I have visions of all my housework getting done, all my writing getting done, and all the laundry magically folding itself into neat little piles and floating to the appropriate drawers. This last dream may come from watching too much Mary Poppins as a child. And I dream that there are no hard things like people dying, war, disease, arguments, tragedy, or differences of opinion. Differences of opinion make me sweaty. In an easy world, there would definitely be no bills. Bills are the worst. They come at inconvenient times, they get bigger each month, and, worst of all, I have to pay them. I just don't like life when it gets hard.

I spend a lot of time trying to make my life easy. I organize myself. I avoid conflict in relationships. I try to control my circumstances as best I can, lest I be stretched in any way. I have a great aversion to discomfort. I cling to the familiar and reject change. I don't like pain. Maybe it's just me. Or maybe it's our culture. We have coined phrases like "living on easy street" or "living large." It is something we aspire to. Having everything come to us without putting anything into it is what we really want. Our culture used to value a good work ethic, but now it seems that people would rather just play hard instead of work hard. We want all the perks without the struggle.

When I was in high school, my dad was the president of a Bible college.

I visited the college for an on-campus event and cut to the front of the line. The lady who was in charge of registration looked at me a little funny.

"I'd like to register for Campus Day," I told her.

She smiled and said, "Great. Just go to the back of the line, and when it's your turn, we will register you."

"Don't you know who I am?" I asked. I was the president's daughter, after all. My dad ran the show, people.

And she smiled again and said, "Yep, I do, and you can go to the back of the line. I'm sure your dad would say the same." Ouch.

It's not that I was a huge snob. I just thought I deserved privileges. My dad was pouring his life into this place, for goodness' sake. Shouldn't I get to go to the front of the line? I wanted the perks that my dad deserved without actually having to work for them.

If I must be honest, that is how I would prefer to live my life. Moving to the front of the line. Being served by others. Getting what I want when I want it. Not having to struggle or grow or do anything that goes against my nature. This is largely due to Lack-of-Reality Man. I love this guy. I listen to what he says all the time. He is so nice. Lack-of-Reality Man encourages a rich imagination, saying things like, "God wants you to be happy. You should have whatever makes you happy. With a little whipped cream and chocolate sauce on top."

Or, "You shouldn't have to work on your marriage. If you just say that you love your husband, you don't really have to show him you love him or serve him. Go ahead and put yourself first. It will all work out."

Or, "You shouldn't have to struggle so much. Everything should be easy for you. You deserve a break after what you've been through. If something is bogging you down, just get out of it. Life is not supposed to be hard."

And that is the clincher for us tired supergirls. We don't want to believe that life is supposed to be difficult. We know that Jesus promised us trials of many kinds, but we would prefer to think he has limited those trials to the persecuted believers in communist countries. We somehow think that since we know Jesus and we love Jesus, only good things should come our way. That hardship will flee from us. We want to believe there is some miraculous way to live our lives that won't press in on us or wear us down or hurt us. Lack-of-Reality Man encourages this view, and then we easily become disenchanted with Jesus and journeying with him through life when things get rocky and painful. Because we want it to be easy. All of us tired supergirls have hard things in our lives. We have all been wounded by life and are wondering how we can get out from under the hard stuff. We would like the benefits of knowing Jesus without the fellowship of his suffering. But the two go hand in hand.

As the day of Jesus's crucifixion draws near, he begins to prepare his disciples for the coming week. There is no real way to spin this news in a friendly way or make it easy to digest. He has already shared what lies ahead for him when they get to Jerusalem, but they can't quite wrap their minds around it. He tells them that he will be betrayed, mocked, spit on, beat with whips, and killed. But then he will rise again. They don't get it. This is the Messiah. The king. Their savior. They have other things on their minds.

Then James and John, the sons of Zebedee, came over and spoke to him. "Teacher," they said, "we want you to do us a favor."

120

"What is it?" he asked.

"In your glorious Kingdom, we want to sit in places of honor next to you," they said, "one at your right and the other on your left."

But Jesus answered, "You don't know what you are asking! Are you able to drink from the bitter cup of sorrow I am about to drink? Are you able to be baptized with the baptism of suffering I must be baptized with?"

"Oh yes," they said, "we are able!"

And Jesus said, "You will indeed drink from my cup and be baptized with my baptism, but I have no right to say who will sit on the thrones next to mine. God has prepared those places for the ones he has chosen."

When the ten other disciples discovered what James and John had asked, they were indignant. So Jesus called them together and said, "You know that in this world kings are tyrants, and officials lord it over the people beneath them. But among you it should be quite different. Whoever wants to be a leader among you must be your servant, and whoever wants to be first must be the slave of all. For even I, the Son of Man, came here not to be served but to serve others, and to give my life as a ransom for many."

Mark 10:35–45

James and John are so very real. Here is Jesus telling them that soon he will be tortured and crucified, and they ask him for a favor. Will he save them a seat? Will he honor them when they get to heaven? They have struggled. I'm sure being a disciple was not easy. They traveled long distances with Jesus. Sometimes they had no place to stay. They left their families and the comforts of home to follow their master. They want to know if there will be any perks. They feel they deserve some perks.

Jesus lays it out for the disciples again. It is amazing that Jesus doesn't just throw up his arms in exasperation. He has lived with these men for three years, and still they don't get it. He calls the disciples together and tries to explain. He says (tired supergirl paraphrase),

> We get to be different than the kings and tyrants in the world who make themselves feel big by making others feel small. Whoever wants to lead needs to serve. Whoever wants to be like me will endure suffering.

Now this is not necessarily what we supergirls want to hear. We are following Jesus, and we would like some perks. We would like the perfect marriage, the good job, the well-behaved children, and some financial stability. We would like for our relationships with God and others to come easily. We would like to live tragedy free in a world without chaos, bad traffic, or bad hair. We will continue to follow Jesus, but we are a little anxious about the perks. Jesus is not so concerned about the perks that we think we deserve. The perks Jesus values are not the same as the ones we long for, such as a life without any hard things in it.

The perks in our journey with Christ do not include getting to the end of this life without having to struggle. The perk in our journey is that because of our trials and hardships, because we love others like Jesus did, because we choose to serve others instead of promoting ourselves, we get to be more like Jesus.

Paul puts it two ways. First in 2 Corinthians 4:8–10, he says,

> We are pressed on every side by troubles, but we are not crushed and broken. We are perplexed, but we don't give up and quit. We are hunted down, but God never abandons us. We get knocked down, but we get up again and keep going. Through suffering, these bodies of ours constantly share in

the death of Jesus so that the life of Jesus may also be seen in our bodies.

This blows Mr. Lack-of-Reality Man's theories out of the water. Life will be hard. In fact, because it is not easy, other people get to see Jesus in us. That is perk number one.

In Romans 8:16–19, Paul looks at our suffering another way:

> For his Holy Spirit speaks to us deep in our hearts and tells us that we are God's children. And since we are his children, we will share his treasures—for everything God gives to his Son, Christ, is ours, too. But if we are to share his glory, we must also share his suffering.
>
> Yet what we suffer now is nothing compared to the glory he will give us later. For all creation is waiting eagerly for that future day when God will reveal who his children really are."

Perk number two may be hard to fathom because it means we have to focus on something other than the here and now. We have to realize that we are living our lives out in the light of eternity. Our reality is that this life will be difficult. That is not something we supergirls like to think about. But our other *other* reality is that when we follow Jesus, when we give up our lives to live the life he has created for us, we get to be a part of his family. Forever. On top of that, we get to share his treasures. Perk number three.

> For God has reserved a priceless inheritance for his children. It is kept in heaven for you, pure and undefiled, beyond the reach of change and decay. And God, in his mighty power, will protect you until you receive this salvation, because you are trusting him. It will be revealed on the last day for all to see. So be truly glad! There is wonderful joy ahead,

even though it is necessary for you to endure many trials for a while.

1 Peter 1:4–6

This life may not look the way we want it to look. It may not be full of comfort and ease. But Jesus offers us something we can't get here on earth. We are going to have to hold out and hold on to him through all the crazy hard times until we reach his glorious kingdom. We may not get to sit in the fancy chairs right next to Jesus; that's up to God. But priceless inheritance? Salvation? Wonderful joy? Those are some perks a tired supergirl can look forward to.

# 16
# I DON'T LIKE
# TO ADMIT I AM WRONG

I know a lot of mindless trivia. Many fascinating details and dates, historical facts, and gossipy tidbits reside in the gray matter in my head. I enjoy sharing them with others, even if they may not particularly enjoy hearing them. I know that "tatonka" means "buffalo" in the Sioux language. I know this because I saw *Dances with Wolves* six times when it came out. I had a thing for Wind in His Hair, one of the Indian warriors. (This was all pre-hubby, of course.) I know that in Iceland people get their last name from their father's first name. My name would have been Susanna Richardsdottir (daughter) if I had been born in Reykjavik. My brother would have been Christopher Richardson. Interesting, isn't it? I know that the Aztecs used cacao beans as currency, and their kings drank a chocolate drink that was thought to be from the gods. I, too, think that chocolate is one of God's greatest gifts. These were smart people. I have many more nuggets of knowledge tucked away in my tired superbrain.

I am very sure of all of these bits of information. Pit me against anyone in a game of trivial knowledge, and I will spew obscure facts like a fountain. I will exult in it because I love being right. I love knowing that I have the correct answer hidden somewhere within me and I can trumpet forth with it at any moment. Now, if by chance, I get it wrong, which has been known to happen, I have a terrible time admitting that I am wrong. I don't like saying those words, "I'm wrong!"

It comes much more naturally to say, "Yippee! I am right! I win! I win! I win!"

And even if you have proved me wrong, that there is another answer than the one I have given that is printed on the backside of the card you are quizzing me with, or you drag me to the computer and search seventeen different websites say that you are right and I am wrong, I still may doubt you. I still may feel that inside I am right and that even though you have the power of the entire World Wide Web on your side, you are still wrong. If by chance you convince me that you are right and I am wrong, I will probably want to throw something at you. Like that card you are waving in my face with the right answer on it. So once you have proven me wrong, you may want to hide yourself away for a few months. I don't know why it is so hard for me to admit I am wrong, but it is. That's just me. I guess I'm a teensy bit stubborn.

It's no different when someone comes to me with an issue they have with me. Telling me that I've hurt them or questioning my motives for a certain action. It's no different when I make a mistake with my little guys or do something that hurts Scott, not loving them the way I should. I don't want to admit I am wrong. I don't want to say that I blew it and I need forgiveness. Even when the Holy Spirit brings to mind an area of my life that needs working on or a relationship that needs reconciling, I would prefer he butt out. Really. I prefer to turn a blind eye to my sin. Then I just pretend I am right anyway. It's so much easier than humbling myself, asking for forgiveness, and letting God shape me into the person he wants me to become.

We tired supergirls like to be right. We certainly don't want anyone telling us how to live our lives. And if we have spent our lives thinking one way, we don't want anyone telling us we are wrong. Really we don't. We are not hankering after the truth at all costs. We would simply like to be left alone to do things our own way, even if how we are doing things will lead us to failure or heartache or mayhem. Even if you think you can convince us supergirls that you are right and we are wrong, we don't want to hear it. We like things the way they are. And if you insist on proving you are right, we might throw things at you.

This is in part because of our love affair with Miss Right. We like her so much because she is always telling us how right we are.

"You are absolutely right to be angry with your husband. He made a mistake. You were right. Doesn't it feel good to be right?"

Or, "They may think you are wrong. Maybe in their minds you are wrong. But really you are right. You are always right. Don't admit anything. Stand firm in your rightness."

Or, "Whatever you do, don't examine your own motives or your heart. Even if you think you are wrong, you need to put up a strong front. If you admit you are wrong, they will just use it against you."

More than anything, the Pharisees loved being right. They loved their traditions, their laws, and their sacred practices. They loved the Sabbath a whole lot. They went out of their way to never violate the Sabbath. And then Jesus came along and started healing people on the Sabbath, for goodness' sake. Right out in the open, he healed people. The Pharisees even suggested he heal people some other day of the week. Jesus offended their law-abiding sensibilities. It came to a head when Jesus healed a man who had been blind from birth. His friends took him to see the Pharisees. And it just so happened that Jesus had healed him on, you guessed it, the Sabbath.

The Pharisees asked the man all about it. So he told them, "He smoothed the mud over my eyes, and when it was washed away, I could see!"

Some of the Pharisees said, "This man Jesus is not from God, for he is working on the Sabbath." Others said, "But how could an ordinary sinner do such miraculous signs?" So there was a deep division of opinion among them.

Then the Pharisees once again questioned the man who had been blind and demanded, "This man who opened your eyes—who do you say he is?"

The man replied, "I think he must be a prophet."

The Jewish leaders wouldn't believe he had been blind, so they called in his parents. They asked them, "Is this your son? Was he born blind? If so, how can he see?"

His parents replied, "We know this is our son and that he was born blind, but we don't know how he can see or who healed him. He is old enough to speak for himself. Ask him." They said this because they were afraid of the Jewish leaders, who had announced that anyone saying Jesus was the Messiah would be expelled from the synagogue. That's why they said, "He is old enough to speak for himself. Ask him."

So for the second time they called in the man who had been blind and told him, "Give glory to God by telling the truth, because we know Jesus is a sinner."

"I don't know whether he is a sinner," the man replied. "But I know this: I was blind, and now I can see!"

"But what did he do?" they asked. "How did he heal you?"

"Look!" the man exclaimed. "I told you once. Didn't you listen? Why do you want to hear it again? Do you want to become his disciples, too?"

Then they cursed him and said, "You are his disciple, but we are disciples of Moses. We know God spoke to Moses, but as for this man, we don't know anything about him."

"Why, that's very strange!" the man replied. "He healed my eyes, and yet you don't know anything about him! Well,

God doesn't listen to sinners, but he is ready to hear those who worship him and do his will. Never since the world began has anyone been able to open the eyes of someone born blind. If this man were not from God, he couldn't do it."

"You were born in sin!" they answered. "Are you trying to teach us?" And they threw him out of the synagogue.

John 9:15–34

The Pharisees loved Miss Right. She was their best friend ever. They didn't want to admit that there was the slightest possibility that Jesus could be sent from God. Here was this blind man, healed, standing before them, a testimony of Jesus's amazing grace, and they refused to believe Jesus was the real thing. They didn't want to believe this man would see. Except that he could see and he was schooling them in the things of God. He even mocked them, asking them if they wanted to be Jesus's disciples too. You know they wanted to throw something at him. Instead they got so mad they threw him out of the synagogue.

Throughout Scripture, Jesus talks about the destructive behavior of the Pharisees. How they are blind, how they are like tombs full of dead bones, how they will be held accountable for their wrongdoing. Because their actions mean nothing without the soft heart for God to back them up. They were all empty action and no heart. They were more interested in keeping the law than loving the world. And that went against all Jesus came to do.

For God so loved the world that he gave his only Son, so that everyone who believes in him will not perish but have eternal life. God did not send his Son into the world to condemn it, but to save it.

John 3:16–17

130

The Pharisees would rather pretend to be righteous than admit the fact that Jesus was right. And because they couldn't trap Jesus or prove him wrong or make him act the way they wanted him to, they decided to kill him. Murder is always a good alternative to being wrong, right?

When we tired supergirls close our hearts to God's truth, to his prodding, to his Holy Spirit bringing things into the light, we kill Jesus all over again. We go the way of the Pharisee, blinding ourselves to his truth. We kill his grace that lives in our hearts, we kill his ability to forgive us, we kill his willingness to move in our hearts and change us. We become just like those religious folk who say all the right stuff and do all the right things, but inside we become hard and dead and, of course, blind. Because when we are blind we can't see what God is trying to reveal to us. If we can't see, we have no idea where we are going. And if we don't know where we are going, we supergirls can't be following Jesus. And that's no good. So it is our job to give Miss Right her walking papers. Admit we are wrong, humble ourselves, and ask Jesus to give us new eyes. And the best thing is, he will. It is what he is longing to do. When we admit we are wrong and say that Jesus is right, we give him the chance to breathe into us. To bring life into our dead rituals, our stubbornness, our longing to be right. We are given a second chance at living. We don't have to be like the Pharisees. And just like the blind man who was healed, we get to sing Jesus's praises, and with a super shout say, "I may not be right about a whole lot of things, but I know this: I was blind and now I see!"

**17**

# I AM NOT SURE OF
# MY PURPOSE IN LIFE

When I was little, I wanted to be a nurse. I read stories about Florence Nightingale and Clara Barton, pioneers in the nursing profession. I liked taking care of people. I was sympathetic. I thought I was born to be a nurse. Unfortunately, I was a little too sympathetic. At the age of fifteen, I had my first day of training as a nurse's assistant in a nursing home. One of the residents was befuddled and crying. Her tears did me in. I began to cry with her. And I didn't stop crying until I got home. Not exactly the type of nurse you would long for at your bedside. So nursing was not for me.

Then I thought maybe I would be a missionary. But after several short-term missions trips and a crazy bout with a parasite, I realized that was not my passion either. Perhaps counseling? I majored in psychology in school. But then the thought of counseling people with so many needs depressed me. Not good. Next? A preschool teacher. I love little kids. While this was a better fit, I was still searching. Retail? Decorating? Import/export? Sales? Nothing fit.

I had always thought finding my purpose in life would be like finding the holy grail. I would know what I was looking for, what I was created for, and I would hunt it down like a treasure and accomplish whatever task it was that God had created me for. Some people are so very sure of who they are meant to be. I always longed for that type of drive and assurance. But ringing up furniture in the mall didn't strike me as being all that purposeful. I was always anxious to find that one thing that would make me special. That one thing that would set me apart and make me unique in God's eyes. That one thing

I could do that no one else could do. But I always came away from my soul-searching confused and unclear. I wanted to be going places, doing things, and instead, I was stuck.

Then I went to a writers' conference. I had an epiphany. This was it. I was supposed to be a writer. My destiny was to be a published author. So I wrote. And I wrote some more. All the while remaining unpublished. I began to read other writers and realized there are some absolutely fantastic writers out there. Really funny. Really insightful. Really a whole lot better than I was. And again I plunged to the unpurposeful abyss. Maybe I am not special. Maybe I will never find what I am uniquely created to do. Maybe I will stumble through life without purpose, leaving no real impact behind.

This conclusion delighted Hazy Girl. She loves to leave us tired supergirls in a fog of indecision. She loves when we are confused by all the options of what we should do and who we should be. She gets giddy when we wander through life feeling purposeless and mediocre. She says things like, "Wow, there really are a lot of people who do things better than you do. That's unfortunate."

Or, "It is really interesting that you thought you might be a singer someday since there are only fifty gajillion other people who can sing better than you. I hear there is an opening at Happy Pretzel at the mall. You better go check it out."

Or, "It doesn't really matter what you do or who you are in life. Just getting through is enough. Maybe you should go to college. Or maybe not. Come to think of it, it probably won't make a whole lot of difference."

We supergirls easily buy into this rhetoric that we don't really have a whole lot of purpose or that we won't ever find that thing that we should be doing. We think our impact on the world is minimal and doubt if anyone will take notice whether we achieve something or not. The thing that Hazy

Girl is so intent on keeping from us is that Jesus is not as concerned with what we do as with who we are. If Hazy Girl can keep us focused on searching for that perfect purpose or deceive us into thinking that the perfect gig is the one around the corner, she has won the battle. She doesn't want us to know that God's tagline is "I am that I am" not "I do that I do." Jesus is far more interested in our character than our career track. If Jesus was concerned about IQ ratings, sales potential, originality, winning personality, ability to make an impact on the world, good looks, or business savvy and political acumen, he would have gone an entirely different route when he picked out his disciples.

Jesus called his twelve disciples to him and gave them authority to cast out evil spirits and to heal every kind of disease and illness. Here are the names of the twelve apostles:

first Simon (also called Peter),
then Andrew (Peter's brother),
James (son of Zebedee),
John (James's brother),
Philip,
Bartholomew,
Thomas,
Matthew (the tax collector),
James (the son of Alphaeus),
Thaddeus,
Simon (the Zealot),
Judas Iscariot (who later betrayed him).

Matthew 10:1–4

I'm not really sure how he went about determining who his followers would be, but four of them were fishermen. There goes the diversity angle. He gathered people from the same area instead of conducting a worldwide competition to see who could best speak on his behalf. He picked a tax collector who was not too high in the popularity polls. He chose a political zealot who wouldn't do a whole lot to win over the masses. Then of course, there was Judas, who would betray him. Not the best choices, from my point of view.

Jesus picked the strangest team. These men would carry his message to the ends of the earth. God's representatives. There was not a single overqualified person on that team. Not one who had personal goals of world domination or higher education. There was not a priest or a leader of the community. In fact, their skill sets seemed to be quite common. But then maybe Jesus was not looking for marketability or the cream of the crop. Maybe Jesus was more interested in raw material. I think he was looking for people he could bend and mold, people who would watch and learn.

Undoubtedly, they struggled as disciples. Yielding themselves daily to Jesus often left them with questions. His ways were not their ways. And yet these are the founders of our faith. The men who went on to heal, to minister, to spread the gospel to the very ends of the earth. Not bad for a few small-town boys. All because they followed Jesus. All because they heard his voice and said, "Okay, I'll give it a shot."

Now the important part that we can learn from the disciples is that despite their green-ness, they were smart enough to know they wanted to spend their days following Jesus. They recognized their own limitations and wanted what Jesus had to offer. Maybe it was the excitement and power that drew them to Jesus. Maybe it was his care of others or his authority. But whatever it was, they all said yes when he called them to follow. When he said, "Follow me," they dropped what they were doing and obeyed.

When Jesus calls us to follow him, we tired supergirls must simply answer yes. At that moment, our true purpose begins to form. It is not so much about following a career path as it is about following the path of Christ. When we say yes to following Jesus, our trajectory changes. We are no longer fumbling around in the dark trying to find out what we will do. We are stepping out in obedience, walking toward the person we will become.

Here we are thinking we are useless and purposeless and indecisive after three majors and two and a half career changes, and Jesus is simply asking us to follow him. We are concerned with the where, the when, and the how, and he is concerned with the who. He is ready to mold us supergirls into something so much more than we are. We can wander about, yearning for purpose, or we can place ourselves into his capable hands. Hands that like to work with raw material. No good potter is going to turn down an opportunity like that.

The potter likes clay in its basest form. He doesn't abhor it because it can't figure out how to break out of its lump-ishness on its own. He doesn't look at the clay and think, *For goodness' sake, why can't you pull yourself together and make something of yourself?*

The potter looks at the clay and sees possibilities. He begins to manhandle it and shape it. The potter really, really loves clay. The potter can accomplish something with clay in his hands. On our own, we are stuck. We are a big lump of unpurposed clay. In his hands, we are chock full of possibilities. And he promises to keep working with us until he makes us into exactly the person he has designed us to be. All this clarity and usability really bugs Hazy Girl. Once we turn our questions, our passions, our hearts over to Jesus, she has no choice but to hit the road. Then again, so do we. We supergirls have quite a journey ahead with Jesus who calls us to join him, saying, "Follow me."

And that sounds like we are going places.

**18**
# I AM A
# PEOPLE PLEASER

It's not that I enjoy second-guessing myself or think I can't make good decisions. But I don't know . . . what do you think? There is this innate need in us supergirls to feel accepted and affirmed. It comes, I think, from that thing deep within us that aches to be loved. It would be fantastic if everyone liked us and was happy with everything we ever did. But that is just not reality. So for those of us supergirls who live to please, life becomes a road fraught with anxiety and disappointment. If people don't like us, we can't seem to get happy.

Take, for example, the garbage man. I would like him to think that I take care with the garbage. Or that I'm a good recycler. I try, but sometimes I forget to recycle. I put my plastic, my aluminum, my paper all together. In the trash. And then on Tuesday mornings when the garbage man comes to collect my trash, I cringe inside. Because I know that he knows that I am an unrecycling monster who is polluting the earth and refuses to take a few minutes from her day to walk outside and sort her trash. So if I feel this deeply about what the garbage man thinks, you can see the dilemma that I have when it comes to pleasing the people that I actually come in contact with. Even as I am writing this, I'm wondering if you will like what I write or think it is drivel.

Does the people pleasing never end? Nope. There are so many people we want to like us. We want to please our parents, boyfriends, husbands, children, teachers, neighbors, bosses, sisters-in-law, co-workers, random mall workers, customer service representatives, local coffee shop baristas, pastors, numerous committee members, and the list goes on and on. Why? Because of Miss Do They Like Me?

I'm sure that you know her well. Miss Do They Like Me? is a true blue friend who sticks with you through thick and thin. She encourages you on a daily basis to please everyone with her catchy catchphrase—you guessed it—"Do they like me?"

If you don't base your decisions on her prodding, she says things like, "Oh, wow, now they really won't like you," or "They're probably mad at you."

She is very persuasive. But this is the thing. She is betting her whole game on the fact that you won't realize this small bit of truth . . . there is no pleasing people. That's what makes us people pleasers so terrified.

*They*—whoever *they* are to you—are always changing up the rules. Maybe last week, *they* wanted you to be sweet and demure, but this week it's all about being assertive. Maybe last time you tried to fit in with that crowd, you had to ignore someone else, but this time if you want to fit in, you have to give up your vacation to do charity work in the inner city. Maybe the last time you tried to figure out what *they* were thinking, they liked it when you read your Bible for two hours a day, but this time *they* are saying you should meditate to worship songs. Maybe last month *they* were saying faded-boy-cut-low-rise-jeans and this month *they* are saying super-flare-low-low-rise-don't-bend-down-or-there-will-be-a-show-dark-rinse-who-can-even-wear-those-kind-of-jeans? See what I mean? There is just no pleasing *them*!

One thing I really love about Jesus is that he never let anyone manipulate him. He wasn't concerned about what they thought about him. He didn't let people squeeze him into the mold they wanted him to fit in. When he was dealing with people, he was so sure of himself that he never cracked under pressure. I, on the other hand, seem to crumble at the smallest bit of opposition. What do I think about global warming or teal mascara? I've always wanted the earth to be warm, and I abhor teal. Oh no, wait, what I meant was I abhor global warming and teal is a warm color . . . right? What do you think? I find it hard to stand firm. Maybe it's because I have no idea what I am talking about, I am rarely sure of myself, and I forget why exactly I am here.

In John 6:38, Jesus says, "For I have come down from heaven to do the will of God who sent me, not to do what I want."

Jesus knew exactly what he was doing. Jesus wasn't manipulated; he didn't crumble, because he was all about obeying the Father. It took pleasing other people out of the equation. His whole mission in life is to do what the Father sent him to do and be who the Father created him to be. So it really didn't matter to him when he caused upheaval or pandemonium and when people got angry. He knew he was going where he was supposed to go, doing what he was supposed to do, saying what he was supposed to say. It wasn't easy for him, but he chose it. He chose obedience.

In the Sermon on the Mount, he gave this example.

I will show you what it's like when someone comes to me, listens to my teaching, and then obeys me. It is like a person who builds a house on a strong foundation laid upon the underlying rock. When the floodwaters rise and break against the house, it stands firm because it is well built. But anyone who listens and doesn't obey is like a person who builds a house without a foundation. When the floods sweep down against that house, it will crumble into a heap of ruins.

Luke 6:47–49

So it basically comes down to foundation. Who and what we supergirls build our lives around. Who we believe in, who we listen to, and who we follow shapes the way we walk in this world. Are we living for the approval of *them* or for the approval of the One who created us? Paul asks the same thing of the church in Galatia.

> Obviously, I'm not trying to be a people pleaser! No, I am trying to please God. If I were still trying to please people, I would not be Christ's servant.
>
> Galatians 1:10

Whoever *they* are in your life, the ones you are trying to please, you cannot possibly base who you are on trying to be who they want you to be because, for goodness' sake, it's like building your house on a pile of sand. And all this striving and pleasing others to gain their acceptance or a raise or a bit of peace in your house, it doesn't mean a whole lot because next Tuesday it could all change.

The thing is, when we supergirls follow Jesus, you can hear the meaningless chatter of Miss Do They Like Me? fizzle out. The foremost question in our minds shifts to "Is this what God wants me to do?" And the beautiful thing about God is that his thinking doesn't change. His ways do not change. So we are not trying to shift back and forth to please people who are fickle and ever changing, we are digging in and building our lives around the One who is never going to change. And we get to stand firm in the foundation of obeying Christ, listening for his direction and living free.

I love how singer/songwriter Sara Groves speaks truth through her songs. The truth about living free. The truth about walking the journey the way we were meant to. She's a supergirl who doesn't play. She sings a song about this journey. Instead of losing herself trying to live for others, she is choosing to live out her journey for an audience of one. Instead of being broken down in the pursuit of pleasing others, she is choosing to live and breathe for Jesus. Now that's some good thinking on her part. It doesn't make a whole lot of sense to spend our lives living for others, when Jesus is the only one who gave his life for us. When we are living to please the One who created us, inevitably, we will be living the life we were created for. And that is something a tired supergirl can get happy about.

# 19
# I CRY A LOT

I might as well lay it out. I cry. A lot. I cry about all sorts of things. Sad things. Happy things. The first wail of a newborn baby. My little boys covering me with their kisses. Feeling misunderstood. Scott telling me I am a good wife. Laughing really hard. Documentaries on the Rwanda genocide. Notes from my mom. Encouragement. Loneliness. Sympathy. Disappointment. Injustice. Seeing my college girl-friends at a wedding—supergirls, every one of them. Wearing maternity jeans *after* the baby is born. Seeing someone make fun of my son. A lot of tears reflecting a lot of different emotions. The happy cry. The sad cry. The mad cry. The if-you're-not-nice-to-my-kid-you're-going-down cry.

But I prefer to cry alone. If I do cry in front of someone, it is usually my husband. He is my go-to guy when it comes to crying. Like most supergirls, I don't want others to know my weakness and my pain. I would rather talk about my hard times when I am on the other side of them, triumphant and healed.

Last fall, I visited my cousin Gretchen, who is a supergirl in every way. She had recently had a baby, and I was still reeling from a violent bout of postpartum depression. A year of sadness. Usually when we are together, we laugh, drink cups of hot tea, and tell stories about our kids. We kick off our shoes and enjoy each other's company without pretense. But as we started chatting, we began speaking of the darkness and how life feels too weighty to hold up on the hard days. I began to unravel. With deep sobs, I told her about how my heart hurt and how I could not see any brightness in the near future. I told her about how life was overwhelming me and I didn't know how to work my way out of the pit. I shared my anger, my confusion, and my hopelessness. I cried about the rough places I didn't know how to overcome and confessed that I felt like I was failing my husband and my kids.

She listened. And she hugged me. She was with me in my ache. It was good. She prayed over me, for me, and with me. But as I drove back home, I began to feel embarrassed about how I had collapsed. I felt a little foolish at the depth of emotion I had revealed, and I wondered how I could backpedal over that scene. How I could make excuses for myself. I would have to call her and tell her it was my hormones. Or maybe the building sleep depravity? There had to be some clear reason for my breakdown. I would think of something. I could hardly bear for my cousin, one of my closest friends, to know how undone I truly was. I couldn't possibly be that vulnerable, that wounded, and have her think it was just, you know, me.

There are few things more soul baring than sitting with someone while you sob. While you cry over a job interview gone awry or a boyfriend who cheated on you. While you grieve over a loved one or the death of a dream. While you mourn your first speeding ticket or buckle under a month's worth of stress. Crying with someone is intimate and soul baring.

Why is it that we supergirls have trouble showing who we truly are? Why are we so afraid to share with others, even the ones who love us most, what touches our hearts and crushes our souls? We fight back the big lumps in our throats and blink fifty times per second to keep the tears corralled. Why do we choose to cry alone? Well, for one thing, very few of us cry pretty. There are the puffy eyes, splotchy cheeks, pink faces, runny noses, various squawks, hiccups, the after-crying shudders, crumpled foreheads, and do I really need to go on?

And then there is the fact that crying is a window into our souls. Our tears show people what really matters to us. If we let people see our tears, they get to see the real us. Tears strip away pretense, and all that is left is the truth of who we are and where we are at.

I think a mixture of pride and fear keeps our tears in check. We want to appear in control, and we are deathly afraid of showing our hearts and our passion to those around us. It wasn't always this way. As kids, crying was the way we made our feelings known. We cried to show we were hungry, tired, hurt, or even bored. When puberty hit and those hormones kicked in, we budding supergirls went into crying overdrive. I remember standing in front of my closet at the age of twelve, sobbing hysterically at my ugly apparel. Was there no beauty in the world? Or when I saw the first boy I ever kissed playing ping-pong with another girl. This was real stuff. I felt it deeply. It mattered. The only way I could power through it was to cry it out. Lots of lonely, sad, hot tears and some badly written poetry got me through junior high and high school.

But somewhere in the growing up, Sister Stoic made herself known. She would sigh, "Aren't you just a tad overly emotional?"

Or, "There you go again—out of control. You are really letting yourself go."

Or, "Do you see how they are looking at you? Pull yourself together."

We supergirls really would like to cry, but we feel that crying belies a weakness in us. It hurts to let people know we are hurting. The vulnerability costs us too much. We want to be strong. We think if we cry, we give our strength away to whoever or whatever causes our tears.

So we hide our tears. We refuse to cry in front of the boys who shattered our hearts. We don't let our roommates know that we ache inside when they choose other friends over us. We sharpen our wits to joke our way through painful moments. When depression sets in, we separate ourselves until we can present ourselves whole. We can't bear the thought of breaking down in front of someone. We shove the emotion down deep and hold it in. We make ourselves a few allowances, like chick flicks or our wedding day, but for the most part, we keep the crazy under wraps. .

And the funny thing is, we are just as uncomfortable with other people's tears. Awkward. Who knows what to say? We tired supergirls can barely handle our own tears, let alone others. We feel overwhelmed by their pain and our inability to help them. This reinforces our belief that we should just keep our tears to ourselves. We don't want to overwhelm others with our aching hearts. We want to be women who are calm. Women who fall apart are not quite so super. Isn't the phrase "crying supergirl" an oxymoron? And really, who will love a crying supergirl?

Jesus. Jesus will love a crying supergirl. And he knows how to comfort a crying supergirl, because he gets it. Jesus cried. And he was a man, for goodness' sake. Not to mention the creator of the universe. The Scriptures say he wept. Not a little sniffle. Weeping means a good, hard cry.

Jesus cried when his friend Lazarus died. Lazarus and his sisters, Mary and Martha, were his good friends. He spent time at their home eating with them and teaching in their living room. He loved them and they loved him. I can only imagine the thoughts that went through his mind when he heard about Lazarus's passing. He made his way to his friends' house at the most aching, sorrowful, gut-wrenching time in their lives. The story goes like this:

> When the people who were at the house trying to console
> Mary saw her leave so hastily, they assumed she was going

to Lazarus's grave to weep. So they followed her there. When Mary arrived and saw Jesus, she fell down at his feet and said, "Lord, if you had been here, my brother would not have died."

When Jesus saw her weeping and saw the other people wailing with her, he was moved with indignation and was deeply troubled. "Where have you put him?" he asked them.

They told him, "Lord, come and see."

Then Jesus wept. The people who were standing nearby said, "See how much he loved him."

John 11:31–36

Now I don't think Jesus was crying over Lazarus. I have a sneaking hunch he knew in just a few moments he would raise Lazarus from the dead. I'm thinking he knew that was the plan all along. So why would he cry? Why was he so troubled? I think he cried with his friends. He felt what they felt and he was moved by their pain. He didn't mock them. He didn't shut them down. He didn't excuse their emotion as foolishness. He joined them. He lived with these people, and what was important to them was important to him. Jesus is passionate about people. They are what matters to him. He was compelled to tears on Mary's behalf. He loved Mary when she was crying and shared her pain with him. And he is ready to love a crying supergirl and share her pain too.

Tears aren't shameful. They are real. All the emotion that weighs us down seeps out of our eyes and somehow we are able to let it go. We are passionate supergirls. And we really, really feel things. It is part and parcel of womanhood. And Jesus is good with that. When he was filled with sorrow, he cried. The savior of our souls wept over Jerusalem. He cried about things that mattered, like people's souls being far away from him, and his friends mourning over their brother's death. His tears didn't show his loss of control, or that he just could not manage to hold himself together. His tears showed his realness, his vulnerability because he loved people. His tears didn't point to his weakness, they cracked the window so we can see his soul and his commitment to humanity. Jesus doesn't hold back where we are concerned. He is going to give us everything he has. His truth. His tears. His life.

How can we supergirls offer any less? We are in this thing with him. We are committed to living our lives out in truth and vulnerability and realness, with ourselves and with each other. As for Sister Stoic, she only encourages a facade. It's all smoke and mirrors. She would like for us to cover up our hearts so we don't have to share ourselves with others. Remember? Keep the crazy under wraps.

I never did make that phone call to Gretchen to make excuses for why I was so broken. I think I knew in my heart of hearts that Gretchen knew I was broken even before I began to cry. She would have seen right through my excuses because she has a knack for seeking out truth and clarity. And at that point in my life, I needed to be known for who I was. And she was willing to sit with me in that place of pain, cry with me and love me. Just like Jesus does.

Jesus said, "I have come that you may have life and life more abundantly." Not a fake hold-it-in-don't-shed-a-tear life but a real-vulnerable-sharing-yourself-with-Jesus-and-others abundant life. He is about tearing down walls, about living truth and being himself. He is about lending his strength to those who are weary and crying with those who are crying. So if you feel a good hard cry coming on, grab your tissue, tired supergirl, and know that you are not alone. Jesus, the author of the universe and lover of your soul, is about living life with you. He loves when you are being real with him, no matter what that "real" looks like at the moment. He will never leave you nor forsake you. Even when you have the after-crying shudders.

# 20
# I COVET THINGS . . .
# LOTS OF THEM

If we tired supergirls must talk about the deep, dark secrets in our souls, and we must, it must be said that I am a coveter of the first order. This isn't a recent development. Thinking back to when this deep longing for other people's things began, I realized it started in preschool. Being a pastor's kid, I grew up in church. Our church nursery had some fantastic toys. My downfall was a pink-and-white-striped jump rope I spotted tucked into one of the preschool cubbies. It was a lovely piece of handiwork, and I knew in my little sullied baby soul that I must have it. I told one of my Sunday school teachers it was mine.

Now let's step back and review what coveting is. It is a strange word for us supergirls. It is not an everyday sinning word like *lying* or *stealing*. I can't think of the last time I heard anyone say, "Oh, I really covet that" or revealed to a close friend, "My main struggle in life is covetousness."

It could be because the word *covet* is a bit King James-ish. But I think it is also because our culture thinks it's okay to want things that belong to other people. Whether it's a lamp from Pottery Barn or someone else's boyfriend, if you really, really want it and you absolutely know it will make you happy, our society seems to think you have a right to try to go out and get that thing. Which brings me to the other point of coveting. Coveting spawns other sins. It is the slippery foundation to which we add layers of lying, stealing, scheming, and all other things unholy and very unsupergirl-like.

Back to the pink jump rope. When I brought it to the car after children's church, my mom asked me what I had in the bag. (Being the smarty pants that I was, I had hidden it in a paper bag.) I told mom the children's church coordinator had given it to me. Then my Mom got all excited, thinking it was perhaps a banana cream pie, because this person was famous for baking fantastic banana cream pies. But, no, it was not a banana cream pie. And when my mom thanked this person for giving me a jump rope, the jig was up. Obviously, I was not yet smarty pants enough to realize how everything would go down once the truth was out. I lost out on the pretty jump rope. I was punished. I think the Sunday school coordinator was distraught that I had woven him into my web of deceit, as was the Sunday school teacher. I think even my parents were surprised to see how many adults I had involved in my jump rope highjacking.

Now the good news is, in my case, I don't steal anymore. I think I have battened down the hatches on lying. But the coveting seems to be part of the fabric of who I am. I am so wrapped in it, I don't even recognize it. And Miss You-Deserve-It? She's my best buddy. Everything I see that I want or feel that I should have, she thinks I need and deserve too. She constantly suggests things that would make my life more pleasant. She really is all sweetness and light. She just wants my life to be the best that it can be. Funny thing is that she usually strikes when I have not a penny to my name. It is often after the paycheck has been spent on bills and doctor visits that she beckons me to Target and shows me the wide array of wares that are on sale. Because the Miss You-Deserve-It that lives in my head is a bargain shopper and she is out to save me money.

Scott has talked to me about my bargain mentality, but I just can't seem to grasp the fact that there will *always* be a sale. That word *sale* and its cousins *clearance* and *75 percent off* are my love language. I tell myself that sea blue votive candleholder marked down to $6.98 will make my mantel stunning. My mantel is fine, but not fabulous; it's just miss-ing that little pop. We all need a little pop in our lives, don't we? And Miss You-Deserve-It pipes up, "It's been a tough week. You deserve it. Put it on the credit card. You can pay it back the next time you get paid."

See, Miss You-Deserve-It and I are all very thrifty and rational in my head. But I realized the other day that while I thought they were gone, the lying and stealing are still there. They have just taken on a new form. Although, I would like to think I will pay off the credit card, it rarely happens. Some other bill always comes up. What is really happening in those moments of internal discussion is that instead of lying to a Sunday school teacher and stealing from some innocent preschooler, I am lying to myself and stealing from my future. From my family. Because I am adding to our debt. In this light, that votive doesn't seem quite so beautiful. It could be burned up before it's paid off. And I won't really enjoy it as much as I should because things just aren't as pleasant when they aren't come by honestly. Every time I look at my mantel and see that votive, I think of my big fat credit card bill. And that's not so fun. It makes the pop fizzle.

Some supergirls covet votives. Some covet cars. Some covet jobs or promotions. Some supergirls covet relation-ships or other people's husbands. Some covet houses or family life. Some supergirls covet their friend's ministry or their gift of communication. Some covet cash, some covet security. Some covet friendships and some covet education. There is no limit to our coveting. We supergirls all want more than we have been given.

We want more money, more space, more time, more muscles, more friends, more shiny lip gloss with lip plumper for this season's bee-stung look. Is there anything wrong with that? There are so many things that other people have that we would like to have for ourselves. And we are just trying to be resourceful and meet our own needs. We know that God has created us for more than we are and more than we have at present. And the things that we long for are usually good things. But the not-so-good thing about coveting is that it embraces a lifestyle that is the exact opposite of the lifestyle God would have us tired supergirls embrace. He wants us to love. And coveting is the opposite of loving. There are two great commandments that Jesus tells us to live by:

To love the Lord your God with all your heart, soul, and strength and love your neighbor as yourself. And the loving part sums it all up. Paul talks about it like this,

> Pay all your debts, except the debt of love for others. You can never finish paying that! If you love your neighbor, you will fulfill all the requirements of God's law. For the commandments against adultery and murder and stealing and coveting—and any other commandment—are all summed up in this one commandment: "Love your neighbor as yourself." Love does no wrong to anyone, so love satisfies all of God's requirements.
>
> Romans 13:8–10

Now the adultery, the murder, the stealing, those we get. We tired supergirls understand that you can't really love someone if you are cheating on them, killing them, or taking their stuff. But Paul includes coveting in that group too. You can't love someone if you are pining for what is theirs. You can't be full of love if you are desperate for someone else's boyfriend or their Coach bag. You can't be full of compassion if you are dying over the fact that your co-worker got a promotion and you didn't. And most importantly, you can't love God if you are hurting one of his kids.

Now this I get because I am a mom. When I see someone being mean to one of my kids, I would like to knock them sixty ways from Sunday. It is that she-bear mentality that lurks just under the surface of every mother. Touch my kid and you are going down. That is just how it plays out. Now if my own kids hurt each other, that is doubly painful because I have this great love for both the hurt-er and the hurt-ee. I want my boys to love and care for each other, to see the value in each other and respect each other. And God is our heavenly Father. He has all these kids that he loves day in and day out, and more than anything, he wants us to play nice.

And here's the thing. It is in us supergirls to want things that are not ours, things that don't belong to us, even things that will do us no good whatsoever. We want these things because we have sullied souls. But we also have a God who loves us and has offered us an alternative to getting all tied up in knots over having what is not ours. Later in that same passage of Scripture in Romans, Paul reminds the believers,

> But let the Lord Jesus Christ take control of you, and don't think of ways to indulge your evil desires.
>
> Romans 13:14

Because if we tired supergirls must talk about our evil desires, and we must, we also have to talk about the fact that we have a choice. We have the choice to indulge our evil desires or to indulge Jesus. When we can't control ourselves, we can ask for Jesus to take control of us. We can stand in front of that lovely sparkly blue votive that is seductively whispering our name and say, "Jesus, I am having a crisis here. I am very likely to indulge two or three evil desires, and I need your presence right here in the middle of Target. I need you to control me. And I also need you to control me as I pass by the sweaters that are half off and the chocolate bonbons in the market section."

And with Miss You-Deserve-It screeching in your ear, you may not believe it to be so, but Jesus will give you the strength and fortitude to step away from the votive. He might even go so far as to put a little thought in your head that you would do well to step away from Target altogether, say for two or three weeks. And you might also have the thought that it would be a good idea to share with a friend or sister or husband that you are struggling with said blue votive, that you don't know if your life can be complete without the blue votive and its sparkly goodness, but you think Jesus has other plans for you besides the blue votive and you could use a little backup, a little accountability, when it comes to driving down the street that Target is on because your car could end up pulling into the parking lot of its own accord.

We tired supergirls like to keep our evil desires on the down low. But when we bring our coveting out into the open, share it with a trusted friend, bring it before the most high God, it begins to lose its hold. When we are able to tell another supergirl, "I think Lulu's boyfriend is hot and I'm really embarrassed about it, but I can't stop thinking about him."

Or, "I only have three people in my Sunday school class that I am teaching, and Erma Rosencrantz has forty-two, and I am thinking of sabotaging her coffee carafe next Sunday so that some of her people will be afraid of her beverages and come to my class instead. Could you pray with me?"

God can begin to do in us that thing which he longs to do. He can calm the chatter of Miss You-Deserve-It so that you can give her what she deserves . . . a good swift supergirl kick. He can fill us up with love for others. He can help us take care of his other kids instead of hurting them. And when we are out of control, he can take control of us and our evil desires. Even ones for pink jump ropes and blue votives.

## 21
# I AM NOT GREAT AT SHARING MY FAITH

In first grade, I polled my class to see who went to church. I was shocked to find out some kids didn't go at all. Being a preacher's kid, I found this incomprehensible. I reported my findings to my teacher, Mrs. Hendricks. I think she was a little tickled and with some prodding admitted to being a Baptist. If Mrs. Hendricks believed in Jesus, wasn't that proof enough that everyone should? That was probably the last time I felt totally comfortable talking about my faith, unabashed and without qualms.

I asked Jesus into my heart when I was five at a Vacation Bible School. I followed a funny puppet in saying the sinner's prayer. It all seemed very black and white back then. "Jesus loves me this I know, for the Bible tells me so." What could be simpler than that? But by the time I was in high school, I was mostly paralyzed by my inability to talk to someone about what Jesus meant to me. I was struck dumb by fear. By the fear of sounding stupid. Of not having answers to the hard questions. By the thought of what my peers would think of me.

And I don't know if you've noticed or not, but in this world of political correctness, the gospel of Christ is totally offensive. It talks about sin and stuff. I was an all-star Sunday school student but was mute in the presence of people who didn't believe what I did. And usually when I breached the chasm of faith, my conversations revolved around the dos and don'ts of my faith, like why my friends shouldn't be doing what they were doing. I remember talking to one friend about why she shouldn't live with a guy before they got married. And I think my response was something profound like, "You just shouldn't."

It's hard to imagine, but I'm pretty sure I didn't bring her around to my point of view.

After I got married and Scott and I were youth pastoring, my faith sharing hit an all-time low. By then, I had lived a bit longer, messed up a bit more myself, and knew that more than anything, what people needed was the story of God's grace and forgiveness. He had changed me and moved me, and I wanted the people in my life to know that same grace and forgiveness. I was trying to hold up the light and all that, in the store I was working at. I had been talking to one friend about Jesus. A lot.

We were praying together. She was really interested in Jesus and what he was about. I was excited because I felt like this was a breakthrough for me too. I had always been so fearful, and here I was opening up and being real and Jesus was coming through. I thought any day she would say that she, too, wanted to be a Christ follower. And then one fateful day over lunch, she thanked me for all my prayer and helpfulness in finding a new path of faith for her as she was now studying Buddhism. I was crushed. I went home to Scott, who had been coaching me through my witnessing, and told him, "I'm not sure what I did or how it happened, but I was trying to lead her to Jesus and instead I led her to Buddha."

"Buddha?"

"Yes. Buddha."

Scott just patted my back. He is a born evangelist who shares his faith regularly. He has led his friends to the Lord, not to other religions. And I felt like a failure. I had failed me, and worse, I had failed Jesus. The Great Commission seemed impossible. How could I go into all the world, making disciples of the nations, when apparently my giftings seem to lie elsewhere? Maybe some of us supergirls should go into all the world and maybe some of us should just stay at home and pray real hard for the other supergirls who know what they are doing.

Some of us supergirls are rock stars at sharing Jesus. Some of us grab our friends by the hand and walk them right through the four spiritual laws onto the path of righteousness and have felt the glory of the Lord shining 'round about us. And some of us supergirls feel like we are terrible at sharing because we don't relate to people who don't follow Christ. Maybe we grew up in the church and our story of faith isn't exciting. Or we grew up outside of the church and our story of faith is too gory. Or we are introverts and speaking up about our faith feels like something akin to dying. Or tired supergirls that we are, even though we are following the Christ and would like to talk about him, we have messed up over and over and feel like we are the last ones who should be sharing anything. That maybe we could, quite by accident, lead someone to Buddha. (Who I'm sure was a nice guy and all but definitely not the creator of the universe and savior of the world.)

This is where Mr. Shut-Your-Mouth comes into play. He is the foul foe who mocks our faith and shames our souls and says, "Yes, of course, by all means, believe in Jesus. Just don't talk about him. Because you really have no idea what you are talking about."

Or, "It's amazing how much you say you love Jesus, but you just can't seem to get it right. You better keep quiet. Praying for your friend is enough."

Or, "It's nice that you want to tell your friends about Jesus, but you've never had any training. Maybe you should go to

Bible college first and then you can really know what you are talking about."

All good arguments from a logical point of view, but not exactly what Jesus had in mind. He chose twelve people to get his message out. He chose to tell the world about himself at a time in history when there was no radio, television, or Internet. Writings were only available to the educated elite. How exactly did he expect his followers to tell the world about who he was and what he had done for them? By talking. By word of mouth. By sharing stories and speaking the words of Jesus. By discipling them . . . a scary Sunday school term that conjures up images of deciphering Scripture in some musty back room of a church.

Mr. Shut-Your-Mouth would like us supergirls to think that sharing our faith and all that God has done for us is absolutely beyond us. And he is going to try to stymie us at every turn. Because this is God's grand plan. For us to tell people about him. That's it. He wants us to be his disciples and to tell others how to be his disciples. And that is going to involve some chatting on our part. So if Mr. Shut-Your-Mouth can keep us from talking, then God's grand plan will crash and burn. Jesus relayed this plan to the disciples in a portion of Scripture we call the Great Commission, which quite frankly sounds so daunting, Mr. Shut-Your-Mouth won't have to work too hard to keep us from talking. I can't tell you the last time I was commissioned to do anything or undertook something great. But this is not how Jesus puts it to his disciples. The story goes like this,

> Then the eleven disciples left for Galilee, going to the mountain where Jesus had told them to go. When they saw him, they worshiped him—but some of them still doubted!
>
> Jesus came and told his disciples, "I have been given complete authority in heaven and on earth. Therefore, go

and make disciples of all the nations, baptizing them in the name of the Father and the Son and the Holy Spirit. Teach these new disciples to obey all the commands I have given you. And be sure of this: I am with you always, even to the end of the age.

Matthew 28:16–20

Here are his followers. They have recently seen their friend tortured and crucified. They are probably still reeling from his resurrection. They have eaten fish with him on the beach, seen him pop in and out of rooms like Houdini, and visited with him off and on for forty days. They've come to worship him, but some of them still doubt. Which we can totally relate to because we supergirls can be great doubters. Even after living life with him for three years, they still don't get it. And he breaks down his grand plan into terms they understand.

When Jesus told them to disciple the nations, I'm sure they were not thinking about poring over Scripture in the musty back room of a temple. As he talked to them about how they had lived together the last three years, he reminded them of what is most important.

"Look here, I'm completely in charge. So now that you get that, go and do what I have done with you for the past three years. Just like I came to you, you have to go to them. Go live life with them. Tell them about me. They are not going to get half of what you say, but keep at it. Go cook them fish on the beach and hang out under olive trees. Go to parties, celebrate, and enjoy life. When things get hard, stick by them. Baptize them in the name of the Father, Son, and Holy Spirit just like you were baptized after you repented and believed in me. Teach them all the things I taught you. And you have to know, you're not in this alone, I am going to be with you forever." (Tired Supergirl Paraphrase.)

163

This was something they could do. This was not beyond the realm of the possible. It was the passing of the torch, but he wasn't deserting them. Now, he knew all their stuff. And they knew that he knew all their stuff. He knew some of them were shy, some were goof-offs, some of them were still struggling with their own faith.

And yet he said, "This is the plan, don't worry, you guys can do this, I am always going to be with you."

And they took him at his word because, after all, here we supergirls are. We know about Jesus because some other imperfect Christ follower took Jesus's mountain talk to heart and told us about his love and grace and we listened. And as for Mr. Shut-Your-Mouth, well, he can just shut *his* mouth because there are a lot of other supergirls out there who need to hear about Jesus. And if there is a group of people who know how to celebrate life, hang out, talk about important stuff, and eat good food, it is we supergirls. Some of our friends may get it and some of them may not, but we're going to keep on chatting because Jesus asked us to. And he promised he would never leave us. Even if you have accidentally led someone to Buddha.

## 22
# DON'T FEEL LOVABLE

I have had a lot of days where I feel very bad about myself. I know things about myself that I would cringe to share. Now that may seem strange since I am laying out oh so many problems that I have here on the pages of this book. But there are things in my past and in my heart that feel too big for me to tell. Some days I feel utterly unlovable. I mess up. I hurt the people I love. I struggle with things that I have struggled with for years. My pants are too tight. I embarrass myself with my inadequacies or lack of knowledge. I yell at my kids. And suddenly I am picking myself apart, bit by unseemly bit. I think to myself, *Why can't I be someone else?* Or more realistically, *Why can't I be the person I want to be? Why do I fail? Why do I sin? Why am I this person?* One thing I do fairly well is remind myself of all the ways I don't stack up. There are days when I just don't like myself. I feel small. I feel worthless. I feel pretty much good for nothing.

As someone who has grown up following Jesus, I know all the Christian jargon, all the verbiage acceptable to those who are trying to find their way on that narrow path, and "I hate myself" is not one of those sayings. You can say "I'm struggling" or "God is dealing with me about a certain issue." Feel free to tell people that "I feel bad, but I am believing God is going to help me" or "I need a new revelation of who God is in my life." But for goodness' sake, if you want to see a brother or sister in the Lord keel over on command, just say, "I have been loathing myself in small increments today. If I could crawl out of my skin, I would. I wish I was anyone but myself. I'm not sure why God loves me, I can barely stand myself." That type of honesty is a conversation stopper. Or a gossip starter, since whoever you shared it with may want to "share" your struggle and "pray" for you with others. So a lot of times, we supergirls keep those types of thoughts to ourselves.

That is in the best interests of the Un-courager. The Un-courager would absolutely love you to focus on your worst self. He skips about gleefully as you rip yourself apart and remind yourself of just how unlikable you are. If you can't think of enough things you don't like about yourself, he will join in the barrage.

"Don't forget, you're awkward in social settings. That is a terrible hindrance."

Or, "You have sinned so much in the last week, I have lost count. Who knew you could be evil so regularly?"

Or, "Don't forget your hair. For goodness' sake, I thought it couldn't get any more limp, but apparently it can!"

The myriad of things that we don't like about ourselves is a real downer.

We supergirls are often paralyzed by our own lack. Our lack of attributes. Our lack of talents. Our lack of good looks. Our lack of knowledge. Our lack of righteousness. We spend quite a few days of our lives feeling "less than." Some of the things we don't like about ourselves could very well be true. You have never seen limper hair than mine on the fourth of July in Washington, DC. But some of the things we tell ourselves, about ourselves, are lies straight from the fiery pit of hell. We are lovable. We know this because God was kind enough to have it written down so that we wouldn't forget. In John 3:16, it says in big red letters, "For God so loved the world." Now I assume, since you are reading this book, that you are a part of the world. And I also checked, and the Scripture does not include the disclaimer "For God so loved the world *except for . . .*" with a list of names. So we are all good as far as that goes. But penetrating that thick skin around our hearts, the one that keeps us from believing rich morsels of truth like this one, is a hard thing. We tired supergirls have spent years defining who we think we should be, what we think we should look like and act like in order to be lovable. And never in all those years of trying to become the perfect lovable person have we actually succeeded. We look at ourselves and there are still so many areas that we wrestle with, so many idiosyncrasies that don't lend themselves to worth, so many traces of sin and ungodliness, that we feel we have lost the fight. We just don't deserve all that love.

All through the Gospels, we supergirls see Jesus loving the unlovables and touching the untouchables. He healed lepers and blind beggars. He cast demons out of tormented people and hung out with sinners and reprobates. But something even more amazing and more fantastic is that his heart was moved by women. Women like us. Women who made mistakes and dealt with sin and their pasts and lived messy lives. In a time and culture where women were low on the totem pole, he honored and valued them.

It must have been crowded in Simon the Pharisee's house. Jesus was swarmed wherever he went. One woman heard he was there and went to look for him. She moved through the crowd in the home, probably followed by a trail of whispers. Because she was that type of woman. The type who did things a godly woman wasn't supposed to do. When she got to Jesus, she broke down. And as she wept, tears falling on Jesus's feet, she wiped them away with her hair. She kissed his feet and anointed them with perfume. I'm pretty sure this was scandalous. A bad girl, crying over Jesus, touching him, kissing him. This did not go down well with Simon the Pharisee, who had so graciously invited Jesus into his home. The weeping was bad enough. The fact that a woman of questionable character was in his home rankled him to his very core. The kissing and the foot massage? He was not going to stand for this.

When the Pharisee who was the host saw what was happening and who the woman was, he said to himself, "This proves that Jesus is no prophet. If God had really sent him, he would know what kind of woman is touching him. She's a sinner!"

Then Jesus spoke up and answered his thoughts. "Simon," he said to the Pharisee, "I have something to say to you."

"All right, Teacher," Simon replied, "go ahead."

Then Jesus told him this story: "A man loaned money to two people—five hundred pieces of silver to one and fifty pieces to the other. But neither of them could repay him, so he kindly forgave them both, canceling their debts. Who do you suppose loved him more after that?"

Simon answered, "I suppose the one for whom he canceled the larger debt."

"That's right," Jesus said. Then he turned to the woman and said to Simon, "Look at this woman kneeling here. When I entered your home, you didn't offer me water to wash the dust from my feet, but she has washed them with her tears and wiped them with her hair. You didn't give me a kiss of greeting, but she has kissed my feet again and again from the time I first came in. You neglected the courtesy of olive oil to anoint my head, but she has anointed my feet with rare perfume. I tell you, her sins—and they are many—have been forgiven, so she has shown me much love. But a person who is forgiven little shows only little love. Then Jesus said to the woman, "Your sins are forgiven."

Luke 7:39–48

This is a hope-giving moment for tired supergirls everywhere. Because Jesus revealed his heart. Jesus was not impressed by rules or keeping up appearances or perfection. He was moved by this woman's humility. She knew who she was and what she had done. He knew who she was and what she had done. She was unconcerned with what the other people in that room thought of her. She knew she had found the answer to her love question. Who would love and accept her? Who would forgive her? Who would see beyond who she was and who she could become? Jesus. And this knowledge brought tears. Tears of repentance. Tears of relief. Tears of love. And Jesus didn't turn her away. He let her minister to him. He let her love him. And then he set her free.

Jesus doesn't love us tired supergirls because of what we have or have not done. What we look like or what we don't look like. Jesus doesn't pick and choose between the holy and the unholy. He loves us simply because we are his. Like a mom loves her newborn baby. She loves that little sweet bit of a thing because that baby is hers. Jesus is the same. Any person who comes, kneels at his feet, and believes in him is his. Plain and simple. Prostitute or Sunday school teacher? His. Thief or banker? His. Liar or history buff? His. We all get to be his. We all get to be loved.

This drives the Un-courager to madness. He does not want us realizing that our worth is based not on ourselves but on Jesus loving us. We may not feel lovable, but the truth is, we are deeply loved. We may have done many things wrong, but when we come to Jesus, he forgives us. The Un-courager wants to keep us in limbo, thinking we have to work for God's love, wasting our energy trying to earn what is already ours. The love has been given. The forgiveness has been granted. In the light of Jesus's love, the Un-courager has to go the way of all liars. He is stomped out by the truth.

The best part of the story is that for those of us tired supergirls who have sinned a lot, for those of us who have made mistake after mistake, we just get a chance to love him more. We don't have to feel condemned by our lack. We get to marvel at Jesus's great forgiveness. Simon the Pharisee didn't get it. He lived his whole life following the rules so he didn't realize the freedom that Jesus offered. He didn't feel like he needed to do anything special to honor Jesus. He didn't even offer him the common courtesy of washing his feet or putting oil on his head. Simon should have been freaked out when Jesus read his thoughts and told him the story of the two debtors. He wasn't bowled over by Jesus, because he thought he had achieved holiness and goodness on his own merits.

This woman saw Jesus for who he was. She might have sinned a lot. Jesus read her mail too. He knew what she had done. But she got what he was about. She got that he was holy while she wasn't. She got that he was perfect while she struggled. She got that he was the only one who could give her what she had been searching for. She knew he was her savior. She was blown away by his love and forgiveness, and she did what Simon should have done. She worshiped him. The Son of the Most High God. She wept before him. She thanked him. She took what he was offering. Love.

So it is with us tired supergirls. Like Simon we can pretend there is some way to achieve lovableness on our own merits. We can invite Jesus into our lives but refuse to recognize him for who he is—the savior of our souls. Or we can get real like the woman with the bad reputation. We can recognize that our worth comes from the fact that we belong to Jesus and that he loves us. And we can follow her example. We can love him back.

**23**
# I HAVE
# A LONG WAY TO GO

I have spent my whole life waiting for *that moment* to arrive. You know what I am talking about. *That moment* is that precise second when everything we have hoped and dreamed of, all that our lives were meant to be and everything we have longed to be comes to pass. And hopefully, it will come to pass on a Friday so that we have an entire weekend to celebrate the arrival of *that moment* and the amazing person we now are. We tired supergirls have been yearning for this moment for years and hankering after that feeling of coming into our own ever since we can remember.

I have talked to other supergirls about this very thing. And they feel the same. *That moment* is just around the corner. We have almost achieved it, and yet *that moment* never seems to come. We catch glimpses of it. We get small tastes of it here and there. But somehow *that moment* eludes us. Somehow we are still the same person we were last Tuesday. How can it be that we tired supergirls feel that at some particular time we will face the masses and crow, "Aha! This is it! Everything has fallen into place. Life is all that it is meant to be and I have become all I was ever meant to be!"

I know it sounds silly. But ever since I was a little girl, I have said to myself, *Okay, when _____ happens, then my life will really begin.* My cousin Beth and I would talk about all the amazing things that would happen to us when *that moment* arrived. These chats began when we were around twelve years of age, and lo and behold, they are still happening. At first the blank was filled with "when I get my ears pierced" trailed by "when I turn sixteen" which segued into "when I go to college" then onto "when I graduate from college" followed by "when I get married" joined by "when I find my life's passion" rounded out by "when I have a baby" and on the heels of "when I get published" which is rapidly becoming "when I hold my book in my hands" not to be trumped by "when I get all my children in school" and "when I perfect my marriage" and "when I love Jesus like I should." The blank is forever changing. Maybe it is because I am forever changing. Or maybe it is because when I round the corner on these events, I still find myself the same.

Several of these milestones have come to pass in my life. Even now, I have large hoop earrings dangling from my ears, and *that moment* has not yet arrived. I am way past sixteen. I have graduated from college, married, and bore three extremely large children, and I am still searching for *that moment.* Each of these moments were moments of great joy and wonderment in my life. I think I have never felt so filled with life as I did on my wedding day. Holding my newborn sons for the first time, staring into their perfectly new wide eyes, and kissing their sweet little necks for the first time go down in my personal history as the highest, headiest moments of my life. These are moments I dreamed of. I even felt fairly happy with myself and who I was when they happened.

But, truth be told, those highs moments are few and far between. A whole lot of regular living goes on in between. Each time I think I have reached the pinnacle, I realize, nope, I'm not quite there. I'm missing something. I am not the person I need to be. I still have so much to learn. This amazing event has happened and yet I am still far from yelling out to the universe, "Take note, people! I have arrived!"

And let's not forget the fact that I struggle. On a fairly regular basis. Those three sweet boys can drive me to anger and madness. They really can. My husband and I discuss things. (We don't argue, we discuss.) I have yet to get a handle on the whole "Christian walk" thing. I get frustrated with the fact that I haven't conquered all my fears and overcome all of my weaknesses. I have lots of issues. (As if you didn't know that.) And just when I think *that moment* is around the corner, it's not. There is yet another hurdle to overcome. Another way in which I need to grow. There is that word. Grow. Growth. Growing. Let's just lay it out, supergirls. "You need to grow" is just another way of saying you are simply not where you need to be in a certain area of your life. You are lacking in maturity. You are little when you really need to be big. You need to be way up there, but no, you are way down here somewhere and if you want to get way up there, you must grow. Change. Reshape yourself. Thrust yourself upward. And I must admit that most days I think I will never get to *that moment.*

You'll-Never-Get-There-in-a-Million-Years Guy loves it when I feel this way. He cheers. He rails. He shakes his finger at me.

"You are so right! You are never going to get there. Wherever there is. You really gave it the old college try. But you just really stink when it comes to changing."

Or, "Wow! I know you thought you were different than last week. But you're not. You have always had a hard time when it comes to forgiving people. You are lousy at it. Just give up."

Or, "You will always be who you are. Don't fight it. It's really too hard to change your nature. You can keep trying, of course. I mean, really, you can if you want to. But honestly [in a low hissing whisper], you will never make it in a million years."

Evil laugh and all, he really is the devil. He is the hope killer. The destroyer of dreams and basher of faith. He is in this thing until the end because he really, really wants to make sure that we tired supergirls give up. That is his goal. To see that we give up. You'll-Never-Get-There-in-a-Million-Years Guy wants to make sure that we supergirls think it is impossible to change, even though we've loved Jesus for all these years and listened for his voice and longed to be the person he wants us to be. He wants us to see all that we will never be. And the thing is, if we are trying to hitch ourselves up by our bootstraps, put our best selves into making our own dreams come true, and pouring ourselves into self-betterment, Million Years Guy is right. Even with all that discipline and self-love and positive talk, it will take more than good thoughts and righteous intentions to grow us up into the supergirls we were meant to be. We need something more.

Jesus was always giving his disciples great word pictures about who he was: the Way, the Truth, and the Life; the Bread of Life; the Son of Man; the Light of the World; the Bright and Morning Star; the Vine, the True Vine. He used examples of everyday things to make people see him in a new, relevant way. I'm sure they had passed by hundreds of vineyards when they traveled with him. Grapes were a part of everyday vernacular. The disciples knew about vines.

> I am the true vine, and my Father is the gardener. He cuts off every branch that doesn't produce fruit, and he prunes the branches that do bear fruit so they will produce even more. You have already been pruned for greater fruitfulness by the message I have given you. Remain in me, and I will remain in you. For a branch cannot produce fruit if it is severed from the vine, and you cannot be fruitful apart from me.

Yes, I am the vine; you are the branches. Those who remain in me, and I in them, will produce much fruit. For apart from me you can do nothing. Anyone who parts from me is thrown away like a useless branch and withers. Such branches are gathered into a pile to be burned. But if you stay joined to me and my words remain in you, you may ask any request you like, and it will be granted! My true disciples produce much fruit. This brings great glory to my Father.

John 15:1–8

And this is where we find our hope, supergirls. This is where our faith lies and where our dreams live. In the vine. This is when we look at Not-in-a-Million-Years Guy and say, "Ha!"

Maybe even "Ha-ha!" Because while we may not be able to change on our own, while we have many, many things we have left to accomplish, and while we may not see how we will ever be who we are supposed to be, that isn't the point. It is not up to us to grow ourselves. To change who we are. To root out the bad and prune back the good so that we can flower and blossom into all the loveliness we are meant for. It is not our job. Jesus is the vine. And God the Father is the gardener. He promises he will prune and grow us into who we are supposed to be. He is not about to let us stay the way we are today. He is determined that we should grow, flourish, and produce great things. Jesus tells the disciples they have already been pruned for greater fruitfulness by the message he has given them. If they will remain in him, then he will remain in them. Well. This is good news. In fact, it is spectacular news because we have been given the same message. The message of Christ's unending love. The message that he comes to find and save the lost. (That is us, tired supergirls.) And if we remain in him, he will remain in us. He says his true disciples produce much fruit. That means they are growing, changing, being the people God designed them to be. And this brings great glory to the Father. If we remain in Jesus, he will remain in us and we will bring great glory to the Father. That is one big fat promise.

If we listen to Million Years Guy, we lose. If we cut ourselves off from Jesus, if we give up and choose to rely on ourselves, we have lost hope. If we are severed from the vine, we won't be able to do a thing. But if we hang on, if we bury ourselves into the very essence of who Jesus is and his plan of salvation, then all we have is hope. Truckloads of hope. Hope upon hope heaped upon an even bigger pile of hope. Because with Jesus, nothing is impossible. He says so himself. And he's God.

We have a long way to go. We are not perfect. We have struggles and temptations and heartache. But all is not lost. We will arrive. Because he loves us and he will not let us stay the way we are. And when we choose to remain in Jesus, despite who we are, Million Years Guy does not have a chance. And as we traverse this narrow way, following after God, listening for his voice, submitting to his pruning, getting strength from his strength, we will have *that moment*. We will look into the face of all eternity, and we will hear these words: "Well done."

And we will be tired no more. With those words, the vile foes of the years, the crazy nemeses, the mind-numbing struggles, and the various heartaches will fall away. So fight on, tired supergirl, wherever you are. Because you have heard the message. Remain in him. Don't let go. Even when it gets harder than hard, *he loves you*. No matter what. And that is something that, surely, we tired supergirls can stake our very lives upon.

# conclusion

From one tired supergirl to another, I commend you for finishing this book. I'm not kidding. Pat yourself on the back or get a manicure. This is no small feat. But as you get ready to tuck this book away on your shelf, I would like you to take a moment and ponder a few things.

First, if you haven't asked Jesus to be a part of your life, there has never been a better time than right now. Find another Christ follower to pray with or simply say this prayer wherever you are. Even if you are in your favorite store. He will still hear you.

Jesus, I believe you are God's Son
    Who came to die for me and rose from the dead so that
I could really live.
    Forgive me for my sins. I invite you into my life.
    I want you to be the boss of my life. I want to follow you.
I need you. Amen.

Now that you have asked Jesus to lead you in your life's journey, make sure you tell someone what you have done. This is important because, really, this is a new beginning and a time to celebrate, probably with a whole lot of chocolate. Other people who follow Jesus would love to walk you through this, encourage you, tell you more about Jesus and who he is and how much he loves you (and share your celebratory chocolate). This is good stuff!

Second, for those of you supergirls who have been following Jesus for quite a while, sometimes it helps to take a look back to where all the tiredness began and how that beginning pertains to our present journey. And that would take us back to good old Eve. When we find Eve in the garden, she is not tired. In fact, being a new creation and all, she is anything but tired. Eve is brimming with life and hope and questions. She is living life in perfect communion with God and Adam. We tend to think it all went downhill when she bit into the apple.

But the story of the tired supergirl began long before Eve succumbed to the first crunchy bite of fruit. The story of the tired supergirl started when Eve began to believe the lies of the Snake. How she took them to heart and believed them to be true even though he was a snake, for goodness' sake. It started with a hiss and a whisper and before she knew it, the thought of what that apple held, the excitement that was buried in its flesh, the new worlds of power and life that it held for her, wormed its way into her heart, and she was hooked. (Sound familiar?) I've often wished that I could have been there in the garden, to screech in a hideously high voice, "Don't do it, Eve! In the name of all that is good and holy, do not listen to that wretched snake! Think of all that pain in childbirth that is headed your way. And mine, for that matter! For goodness' sake, step away from the apple!"

But then you should probably also know that if I had been there, I'm sure I would have beat her to the tree. I really do love fruit, and I also find it very easy to sin. So in some ways

I'm really glad I wasn't there, because Adam and Susanna doesn't have quite the same ring to it. But I digress.

The downfall of tired supergirls, in general, begins with the conversations that flood our minds. Conversations that excite us or feel right or just seem to make sense in the moment. We know about the Snake, thanks to our forebearer, Eve. We know he is sneaky and evil, and we do our best to block out the drone of his oily voice, with its slick lies. But the sneakiest thing of all is that he is a chameleon. He can easily disguise himself. And he is not above using a plethora of underhanded tactics to drown out the voice of the Father. The one that we long to hear and follow. The One who holds the key to all we hope and dream of. So the Snake has come up with a crew of different allies or nemeses, if you will, to aid him in the battle of the mind that he wages against all supergirls. Plan A was to take out God. As we all know, that didn't happen. Plan B is that he wants to take down as many of us as he can with him. He's going to keep us from hearing the Father's voice any way he can. The Snake is playing hardball.

We tired supergirls struggle against the voices of those nemeses on a remarkably regular basis. We truly long to be all that God has made us to be and long to reflect a little bit of God's glory to the world around us. We want to shine some light and close the gap between the person we are at present and the person we hope to become. We want to shut out all voices except the one that matters. The voice of the One who created us.

With a bit of God's grace, I am hoping this book has and will continue to aid you in that journey. That as you read these confessions, some sad, some silly, all true, you found yourself turning Christ-ward, looking to Scripture for his truth and straining a bit harder to hear the voice of Jesus.

And that you found a huge measure of grace poured out over you and are beginning to have some understanding of his unbelievable love for you, just as you are, even with all of your weaknesses and shortcomings. (And also, I really hope that you will be able to do some serious damage to that lousy snake and his stinky lies . . . maybe freeze him with your laser beam of truth or knock him sideways with a gnarly roundhouse kick . . . since you are a supergirl, after all.) So, all that being said, there is just this. Ephesians 3:14–21. It is a prayer, a blessing, that Paul prayed over the church in Ephesus.

I pray the same for you. Please pray it for me.

When I think of the wisdom and scope of God's plan, I fall to my knees and pray to the Father, the Creator of everything in heaven and on earth. I pray that from his glorious, unlimited resources he will give you mighty inner strength through his Holy Spirit. And I pray that Christ will be more and more at home in your hearts as you trust in him. May your roots go down deep into the soil of God's marvelous love. And may you have the power to understand, as all God's people should, how wide, how long, how high, and how deep his love really is. May you experience the love of Christ, though it is so great you will never fully understand it. Then you will be filled with the fullness of life and power that comes from God.

Now glory be to God! By his mighty power at work within us, he is able to accomplish infinitely more than we would ever dare to ask or hope. May he be given glory in the church and in Christ Jesus forever and ever through endless ages.

Amen.

# study questions

**Chapter 1: I am oh so tired**

1. In what part of your life do you struggle with the Tired Lady?
2. How do you feel like life is pulling at you?
3. Do you identify with Peter and his struggles?
4. What is your prayer as you ride the edge of imperfection and are caught on the cusp of crazy living?

**Chapter 2: I am not a supermodel**

1. Do you feel pressure to look a certain way? Where does that pressure come from? From yourself? Your peers? Your family?
2. How do you think God views how you look?
3. Do you give more care to your "inner beauty" or your "outer beauty"?

## Chapter 3: I have pride issues

1. Can you think of a situation where pride has led to your own downfall?
2. In what areas of your life do you struggle with pride?
3. Using the definition of humility, recognizing your-self for who you truly are, how would you define yourself?
4. How does the fact that Jesus loves you, just as you are, imperfections and all, change your view of yourself?

## Chapter 4: I worry about things

1. What does worry rob you of on a daily basis?
2. Why is it so hard to turn to God and trust him with your needs and concerns?
3. Do you believe that God has the ability to meet your needs?
4. How can you change the way you worry about things into a prayer that offers God your concerns?

## Chapter 5: I forget there is no more condemnation in Christ

1. What are the things that you feel condemned about?
2. How can you tell the difference between feeling con-victed about something by the Holy Spirit versus feeling condemned about something by Condemno Boy?
3. What does "free" look like to you when you realize that Christ has forgiven all of your sins and loves you completely?

## Chapter 6: I want chocolate to solve my problems

1. What is your substitution of choice? Is there more than one?
2. Do you identify with the woman at the well who keeps trying to fill her heart with the same thing over and over again but can't seem to find what she needs?
3. What is the hole that you would like Jesus to fill in your life?

## Chapter 7: I sin a lot

1. What sin do you need to bring into the light?
2. How does it make you feel that God is looking for you, wanting to forgive you so that he can hang out with you?
3. Do you have a close friend with whom you can be accountable to and share your sin and your struggles, and support each other in areas of weakness?

## Chapter 8: I am jealous of my friends

1. What things make you jealous?
2. Does your jealousy move you to sabotage others with your thoughts, words, or actions?
3. How do your feelings of jealousy change when you realize the things or opportunities you are jealous of were never meant for you?
4. What are the things in the life God has granted you that you are thankful for? Relationships? Personality traits? Accomplishments?

## Chapter 9: I judge people

1. Do you have the unspiritual gift of judgment?
2. Why is it so hard to examine our own issues, while finding fault in others comes so easily?
3. How do you think your view of others will change if you concentrate on removing the "log from your own eye" before judging them?

## Chapter 10: I have anger issues

1. What really makes you angry?
2. When have you had a hard time controlling your anger?
3. What are some of the ways that you could let God use your anger to motivate you to make your life better? Or to make the lives of those around you be what they were meant to be?

## Chapter 11: I am undisciplined

1. What are the areas in your life where chaos reigns?
2. What disciplines could you incorporate in your life to help you invest in your future?
3. What are some ways that you can say no to yourself that would add to your life?
4. What are the reasons that you want to see past the momentary and look to the eternal by incorporating discipline in your life?

## Chapter 12: I get too busy for God

1. How can you go about having a "devotional life" versus a "devotional time"?
2. What do you think about the JOY song and the idea of putting Jesus first, Others second, and Yourself last?
3. How did Jesus remain so secure in his purpose and remain unmoved by the Pharisees or the multitudes of religious expectations of him?
4. How can you model yourself after Jesus and learn from his dealings with others?

## Chapter 13: I am selfish

1. How often do you struggle with the Diva in your own walk with God?
2. What does your "selfish ambition" look like? What "cross" is Jesus asking you to take up and follow him with at this point in your life?
3. How can you drown out the voice of the Diva so you can hear the voice of Jesus more easily?

## Chapter 14: I am lonely

1. What are you lonely for in your life?
2. Is there a certain relationship that you are longing for at this point in your life?
3. Is it difficult for you to turn to Jesus when you are lonely? Why?
4. How has Jesus met you in your loneliness before?

## Chapter 15: I wish life was easy

1. In which ways do you wish your life was easier?
2. In these specific areas, what do you think God is trying to teach you?
3. What are the perks that you want out of your relationship with God? What does God think about the perks you are longing for?
4. What are some trials in your past that God has used to reveal himself living in you?

## Chapter 16: I don't like to admit I am wrong

1. Is it hard for you to admit that you are wrong or do you find it easy? Why?
2. Is there an area of your life where you would rather pretend you are "righteous" than admit that Jesus is right and change your behavior?
3. Why is it so easy to become like a Pharisee when all you really want to do is follow Jesus?

## Chapter 17: I am not sure of my purpose in life

1. Do you ever struggle with finding your life's purpose?
2. When you look at who Jesus picked to be his disciples, does it give you hope? Why or why not?
3. What do you think "the potter" sees when he looks at you?

## Chapter 18: I am a people pleaser

1. Do you recycle? Do you care if I know you don't recycle?

2. Do you find that you worry more about what people think about you than what God does? Why do you think that is?

3. Who do you want to please the most in your life?

4. How can you build your foundation on Jesus instead of on what others expect or think of you?

## Chapter 19: I cry a lot

1. What makes you cry?

2. What are you passionate about?

3. When was the last time you cried with someone? What was it about?

4. How does your view of being vulnerable and real with others change when you see how Jesus interacted with his close friends?

## Chapter 20: I covet things . . . lots of them

1. What do you covet most? Why?

2. What are you searching for to make you content?

3. How does your covetousness affect your relationships with others? With your family? Friends? God?

## Chapter 21: I am not great at sharing my faith

1. Are you friends with people who don't know Jesus personally? Who?

2. When was the last time you talked to this person about Jesus?

3. What are your fears about sharing your faith?

4. What is your main motivator in sharing the good news about your relationship with Jesus?

## Chapter 22: I don't feel lovable

1. In what ways do you feel lovable? In what ways don't you feel lovable?
2. How does John 3:16 change for you when you substitute your name for the phrase "the world"? (ex: For God so loved "Susanna" that he gave his only Son . . . etc.)
3. Do you identify more with Simon the Pharisee or the woman with the bad reputation?
4. How do you think Jesus feels about you and your "lovability"?

## Chapter 23: I have a long way to go

1. What is *that moment* you are waiting for in your life right now?
2. In what areas of your life do you feel God has been pruning you?
3. In what areas of your life do you feel God is trying to grow you?
4. What hopes and dreams do you have this year as you are following Jesus and growing in him?

**Susanna Foth Aughtmon** is a pastor's wife and mother of three. She graduated from Bethany College with a BA in social science emphasizing psychology and early childhood education. After pursuing various careers, including her own interior decorating business, she decided to stay home as a full-time mom. She assists her husband, Scott, in various ministries at the church they planted in Palo Alto, California.

Join the Fun at the Tired Supergirl Lair!
Calling all tired supergirls: It's time to unite!
Come join the Tired Supergirl Lair at TiredSupergirl.com.

You can:

Check out the latest Confessions of a Tired Supergirl blog

Meet other tired supergirls

Create a profile including your tired supergirl alias! Exhaust-o-Chick, anyone?

Post your own confessions in the forum and talk with other TSGs

Post videos

Hear some of Sue's audio TSG confessions

It's free! Come and join us today. Go to TiredSupergirl .com and click on "Tired Supergirl Lair."